YOUR GOLDEN EARS
FIRST
PIANO
LESSONS
FOR ADULT BEGINNERS

YOUR GOLDEN EARS

FIRST PIANO LESSONS

FOR ADULT BEGINNERS

Learn With 5 Minutes Daily Practice, Master Finger Dexterity & Technique Using Sheet Music, Songs, Music Notation and More!

VOL.1

MUSIC MOUSE STUDIOS

Contents

Introduction

It was a quiet afternoon as Mrs. Thompson strolled down the streets. Aside from the crisp autumn breeze stirring up the leaves at her feet, the only other thing she could hear was the faint sound of piano music in the distance. Mrs. Thompson quickly recognized the tune, as it was one of her favorite Mozart sonatas. In an instant, she was whisked away to her childhood, where she longed for the moment she could sit by the piano and bring forth enchanting melodies. She had always regretted never taking piano lessons as a child, but life had dealt her the cards it did, and she never had the chance to learn.

Have you ever wished, like Mrs. Thompson, you could turn back time and learn to play the piano? Ever hoped that you could entertain your friends by playing some good old piano classics? Maybe you've always wanted to hone your skills so you could one day play piano at your church. Or perhaps you already are a musician and want to expand your skill set by gaining a solid foundation in piano. Whatever your situation is, it's never too late to start your journey to becoming a pianist!

With this step-by-step comprehensive piano course accompanied by online demonstration videos, you can learn in digestible 5 to 30-minute lessons how to read music from well-known classical piano literature, develop finger dexterity and flexibility, gain a deep understanding of music theory, and uncover fascinating insights about the composers and songs you're learning. Written by a music veteran, Andrea Chang, the founder of Music Mouse Studios, Andrea has a dual B.A. in Music Education and Music Composition from the University of California, Los Angeles, and is an alumni of USC's prestigious Scoring for Motion Pictures and Television program. She also is a graduate of the Conservatory of Recording Arts and Sciences. Andrea has composed music and sound design, and led audio teams for video games for over a decade. She has worked on staff at Electronic Arts, Microsoft, and Hi-Rez Studios.

Taking this first step is a decision that you won't regret! It's an experience filled with challenges, inspiration, and boundless joy that will accompany you for many years to come. But, like any new skill, learning the piano takes time, practice, and patience. If you don't grasp it immediately, don't be discouraged – keep practicing, and you'll get there. If you wish to receive further support, please check out our website www.musicmousestudios.com for additional resources; we have a piano YouTube channel providing demonstrations and options to receive individual support. Thank you for entrusting us with your musical education – we can't wait to walk alongside you on your piano journey!

Your Free Gift!

As a token of appreciation for your support, we would like to offer you a special gift. We have curated a collection of songs and sheet music for you to explore and enjoy, featuring a variety of songs that will further enhance your piano repertoire as you continue your piano journey after the final lesson.

To receive this exclusive free download, simply visit https://www.musicmousestudios. com/contact and include the text "SHEET MUSIC" in your message. We hope these musical gems will bring you joy and inspiration. Thank you for choosing our book!

Join Our Community!

The joy of learning the piano is even greater when shared with a community of like-minded individuals. We would like to invite you to join our piano community, where you can connect with fellow pianists, share your experiences, and receive support along your musical path. Engage in inspiring conversations, exchange tips and techniques, and discover new insights from others who are on the same piano journey as you. Together, we can celebrate achievements, overcome challenges, and foster a sense of camaraderie in our shared passion for music.

To become a part of our community,
visit our website at https://www.musicmousestudios.com/community
and join us today!

Pacing

Each lesson is small, digestible, and designed to be completed within, on average, a 5-30 minute timeframe (though some lessons may take longer). If you need to review a lesson from a previous day, we encourage you to do so – repetition is key to reinforcing and solidifying your understanding of the material. If you already have some musical background, feel free to complete more than one lesson a day. This book is intended to be adaptable to learners starting at various "beginner" levels.

The goal is for each lesson to feel like a one-on-one session with a teacher, so some material will be repeated to help review and build upon the concepts you've learned from previous lessons.

Before diving into each lesson, make sure to scan the QR code below to access the accompanying instructional videos or visit https://www.musicmousestudios.com/piano-instructional-videos. These videos will provide invaluable guidance and enhance your learning experience. So without further ado, let's get started!

LESSON
1
Keys to Success

DAY 1

Piano vs. Keyboard: Making the Right Musical Move!

A common question that arises is if one should invest in a piano or a keyboard? Each option presents its own unique set of benefits and drawbacks. Let us delve into the realm of keyboards first.

Keyboard

Advantages

1   Price – A keyboard is more affordable if you have a smaller budget. It allows you to gauge your interest before committing to a full-sized piano. Keyboards typically range from $100-$2,000. Though some digital pianos that imitate baby grands can exceed that range, most keyboards lie within those general ballpark prices.

2   Portability and Convenience – Keyboards are smaller and more portable, making it easy to practice at any time or place.

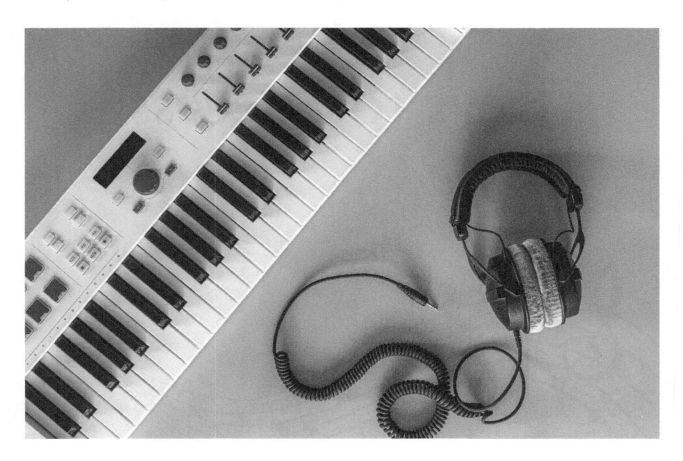

3 Versatility – Most keyboards come with synth patches of other instrument sounds. This introduces you to other instruments and allows you to more easily write your own music, as many keyboards have MIDI capabilities that enable you to plug them into a computer and record the sounds they produce. In contrast, a piano lacks this functionality, and you would need to purchase a microphone and audio interface to record its sounds.

4 Volume control – Many models allow you to adjust the volume up or down or plug in headphones, which is particularly helpful if you're practicing in a location where you can't make much noise.

Disadvantages

1 Finger strength – because keyboards tend to have lighter keys than pianos, often it is difficult for someone who's used to playing solely on the keyboard to transition over to the piano and maintain a consistent, good tone. This generally applies more so to performances. If, for example, you are called to perform your songs on a piano and are only familiar with playing on keyboards, this could be a variable that affects the quality of the performances you give.

2 Technique – While a keyboard can be great for beginners, there may be better options for more advanced players since developing good technique on a keyboard is more challenging. This ties into finger strength but also for more challenging music, such as fast-moving notes or sweeping motions across the piano. These advanced techniques are much more difficult to execute on a keyboard.

3 Overall sound – because the keyboard is an electronic instrument, it won't have the same acoustics as a piano. The piano being a lot larger, has a fuller and more reverberant sound, allowing the pianist to generate a more beautiful tone.

So if you do opt for a keyboard, be sure to choose one with weighted keys, as this will more closely emulate the feel of a piano, helping to build up finger strength and ensuring better control so that you don't accidentally hit a note due to a light touch.

In terms of keyboard brands, a lot of that will come down to personal taste. Yamaha is a solid choice, but I recommend heading to your local instrument store and testing out which keyboard sounds and feels the best to you.

Piano

For those dedicated to playing piano long term, investing in an acoustic piano is the best option. However, acoustic pianos also come at a higher price tag, ranging anywhere from $3,000 to $50,000 or beyond. Similar to keyboards, ultimately, it will also come down to personal preference on the feel and sound of the instrument, but here are some general considerations to keep in mind:

1 Upright versus a Grand Piano

Upright pianos take up less space because they are strung vertically versus horizontally in a grand piano.

Because of that, uprights are also generally less pricey than grand pianos, so if you have a more modest amount of space and budget, I recommend getting an upright piano.

2 The Piano's Sound

Grand pianos are larger and have a fuller sound. If you want that concert experience, a grand piano is the best option. There are baby grands as well as full grands. Baby grands are smaller versions of grand pianos and are usually 5″ and 5′ 5,″ compared to full grand pianos that can range from 5′ 6″ to 9″ for a concert grand.

I suggest visiting your local piano dealer to determine which piano's sound you prefer the most. If a baby grand is similarly priced to an upright, I highly recommend selecting the baby grand, as the fuller sound of a grand piano makes a world of difference.

Though many different brands exist, I am particularly fond of Bösendorfer pianos. Consider whether the sound is brighter or darker when trying out and evaluating different pianos. I prefer slightly brighter pianos, but not so bright that they sound like a keyboard. Ideally, you want the sound to be crisp and clear.

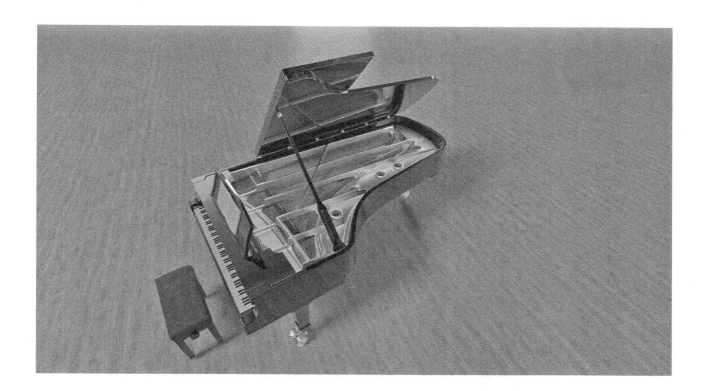

3   The Feel of the Piano

When selecting a piano, it is crucial to assess its sound quality and tactile feel on your fingers, as a piano you can naturally and comfortably play will likely inspire you to practice more frequently. Similar to selecting bowling balls of various weights, pianos also come with keys of different weights. Discovering the ideal key weight that aligns with your preference is essential in finding the piano that brings you the utmost comfort and satisfaction.

Mastering the Piano Layout

A piano consists of white and black keys, and they follow a consistent pattern, alternating between 2 sets of black keys and 3 sets of black keys across the entire piano.

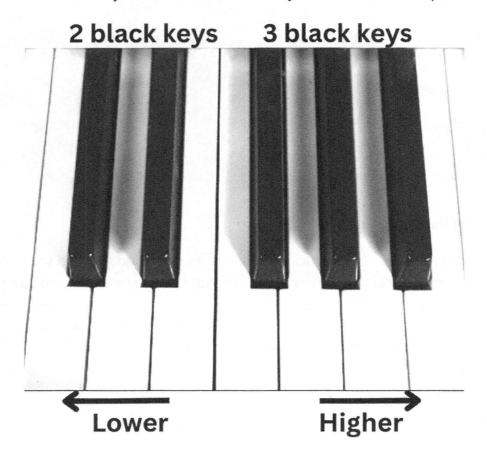

When you move toward the left side of the piano, the notes get lower. When you move to the right side of the piano, the notes get higher.

Playing Exercise

Video link: *https://www.musicmousestudios.com/piano-instructional-videos*

☐ First, try to play all sets of 2 black keys across the whole piano.

☐ Now see if you can play all of the groups of 3 black keys throughout your piano.

C is the first white note underneath the two black notes, as seen in the picture below. We play the note C with our thumbs. Middle C refers to the C positioned right in the middle of the piano. It sounds like this.

Video link: *https://www.musicmousestudios.com/piano-instructional-videos*

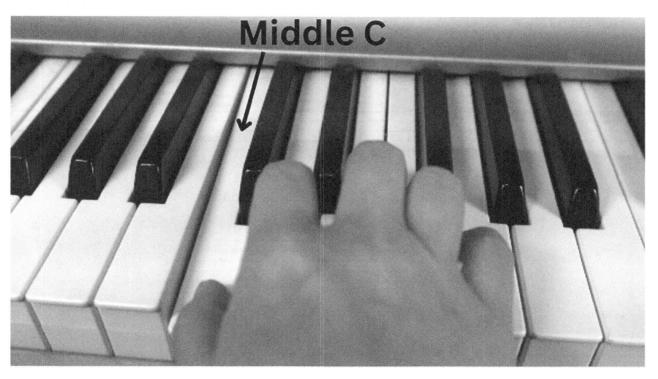

Playing Exercise

☐ Find all the C's on your piano.

☐ Find middle C on your piano.

Decoding Music Notation

When learning a new language, one must master both the written and spoken form. This also applies to music, as it serves as its own language. Learning to read and write music is part of becoming literate and fluent in it. This will create a deeper understanding of what you are playing and make you a better musician who can quickly learn, understand and interpret any piece of music. That being said, let's dive into some terminology for reading and writing music.

As seen below, a staff is what music notes are written on. When counting lines on the staff, we generally count from the bottom up.

Some notes on the staff are on lines while others are on spaces.

Line   Space

Line or Space

In the exercise below, identify whether the note is on a line or space.

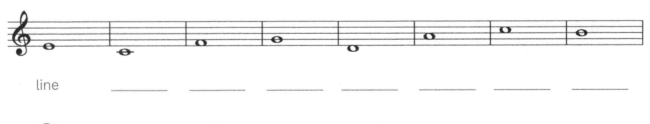

line

Clefs are symbols at the beginning of a staff that show what hand one should play with. As seen below, a Treble Clef signifies to play with our right hand. Notice how the Treble Clef looks like the letter "G," and thus can also be referred to as the "G Clef." Refer to the picture below to see the calligraphy "G's" written next to the Treble Clef.

Treble Clef play with RH

A **Bass Clef**, as pictured below, is placed at the beginning of a staff to signify that we should be playing with our left hand. A Bass Clef looks like an "F"; thus, it can also be called the "F Clef." Refer to the picture below to see the calligraphy "F's" written next to the Bass Clef.

Bass Clef play with LH

First, we will be focusing on just the treble clef. This is what middle C looks like on a treble clef. Notice how it is a line note that is not on the staff but has its own line below the staff. We call this line a **ledger line.**

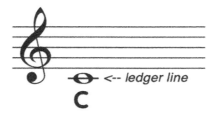

Music Notation Exercise

☐ Draw a treble clef.

☐ Draw middle C.

Within the realm of music, two key elements intertwine: the music notes and the rhythm. We have delved into the music notes, and now it is now time to explore the enchanting world of rhythm.

Exploring the Rhythm Tree

Imagine that there is a big fat egg. This egg is 4 beats and is called a whole note. We cut this egg in half, and we get 2 half notes. Half notes are two beats each, with a little stem going upwards from the egg. We take these half notes, cut them further in half, and get quarter notes. Quarter notes are one beat each, and they look like half notes, except the insides of the eggs are filled in. Then we cut the quarter notes in half and get 8th notes. 8th notes are half a beat each and are connected by a little line in between the top of their stems. Staying true to its name, there are eight 8th notes in a whole note, 4 quarter notes (like 4 quarters in a dollar) in a whole note, and 2 half notes in a whole note. Refer to the picture below to see the full rhythm tree.

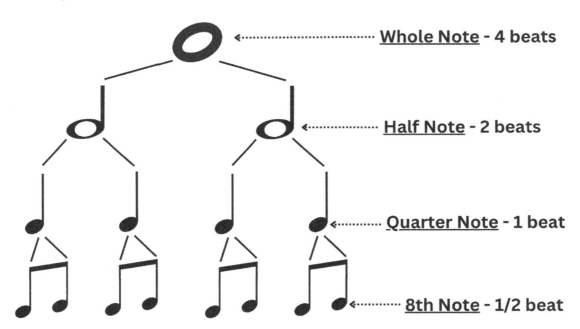

Whole Note - 4 beats

Half Note - 2 beats

Quarter Note - 1 beat

8th Note - 1/2 beat

Note: 8th notes can either be connected like they are above, or they can be single 8th notes. As single 8th notes, they look like this:

8th notes are generally connected together in groupings of 2 or 4 for ease of reading.

Rhythm Exercise

☐ Clap through the rhythm tree for a friend.

Video link: *https://www.musicmousestudios.com/piano-instructional-videos*

Playing Exercise –
Putting it All Together

☐ Write 4 whole note C's below.

☐ Write 4 half note C's below.

☐ Write 4 quarter note C's.

☐ Write 8 eighth note C's.

☐ Play 4 whole note C's.

☐ Play 4 half note C's.

☐ Play 4 quarter note C's.

☐ Play 8 eighth note C's.

Video link: *https://www.musicmousestudios.com/piano-instructional-videos*

Congratulations, you've completed Lesson 1!

You are doing an amazing job! Keep going to Lesson 2!!

"Success is not final; failure is not fatal: It is the courage to continue that counts."

—WINSTON S. CHURCHILL

LESSON
2
The Melodic Prelude

In this lesson, we will deepen our familiarity with the piano keyboard, explore essential music terminology, and enhance our technique through engaging exercises. Get ready to dive in and take your skills to the next level!

☐ Play all the sets of 2 black notes on the piano.

☐ Play all the sets of 3 black notes on the piano.

☐ Play all C's with your thumb.

☐ Find middle C and play with your thumb.

Notes C-G, New Note D

We play D with our second finger, which is the white note next to C, as seen in the picture below.

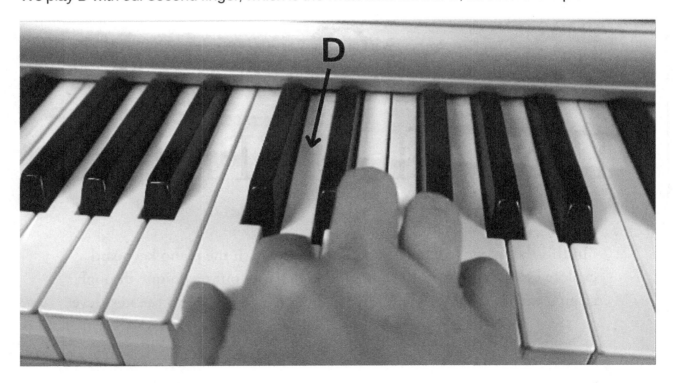

☐ Playing exercise: Play D on your piano.

☐ Playing exercise: Now, let's place all our right hand fingers on the piano. Middle C should be played by your thumb, D by your second finger, E by your third finger, F by your fourth finger, and G by your fifth finger. Play C-G on your piano. Make sure you have the proper hand posture with curved fingers.

Video link: https://www.musicmousestudios.com/piano-instructional-videos

Decoding Music Notation

What does D look like on the staff? In the treble clef, D is below the bottom line of the staff on a space note, as seen below.

What does C-G look like on the staff?

In the treble clef, it looks like this:

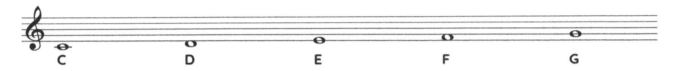

C   D   E   F   G

☐ Music Notation Exercise: Draw a treble clef below and then the notes C to G (like in the example above). Circle D.

Rhythm Exercise

☐ Review: Clap through the full rhythm tree.

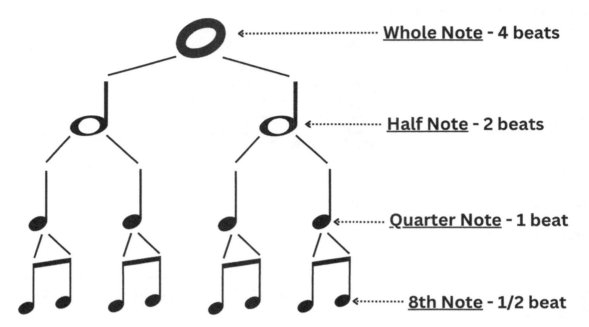

Whole Note - 4 beats

Half Note - 2 beats

Quarter Note - 1 beat

8th Note - 1/2 beat

Measures, Bar Lines, Intervals, Oh My!

DAY 11

Look at the score above. Note that this song has 4 measures. **Measures** are little segments of music broken down by the lines in between the notes. Another name for a measure is a "bar." The lines that separate each of the measures are called **bar lines.**

In the last measure, we see a **chord**, which is when **multiple notes** are played together simultaneously. Chords can consist of any number of notes – 2 notes, 3 notes, 5 notes, etc. Conversely, **intervals** consist of only **2 notes** and are just the number of notes between the bottom and top notes. When the notes are right next to each other on the piano, like how C and D are, this interval is a **2nd** because the number of notes between the bottom and top notes is 2 (C is 1, D is 2). 2nds can occur on any note; for instance, C to D, D to E, E to F, F to G, G to A, A to B, and B to C are all 2nds.

CD
2nd

When an interval is played simultaneously like a chord, it is called a **harmonic interval** since the notes make "harmony" with each other.

In contrast, when the notes in an interval are played successively after each other, we say the interval is arpeggiated or broken and is called a **melodic interval**. The notes are played or sung one at a time like a "melody."

THE MELODIC PRELUDE   19

Playing Exercise

☐ Write down the appropriate letters below the music notes.

MEASURE 1   MEASURE 2   MEASURE 3   MEASURE 4

C   CD

Check to see if you got them right below!

C   C   C   C   D   D   D   D   C   D   C   D   CD   CD   CD

☐ Circle all the barlines. How many measures are there?

☐ Clap and count the rhythm. It should sound like the following.

Video link: https://www.musicmousestudios.com/piano-instructional-videos

☐ Finger the exercise first on the table. For example, the piece starts with 4 C's, so you will hit the table 4 times with your thumb. The following measure has 4 D's, so you will use your pointer and hit the table 4 times. Measure 3 has C, D, C, D, which means you will play your thumb, pointer, thumb, and pointer on the table. The piece ends with 3 chords (CD), which means you will play your thumb and pointer simultaneously 3 times on the table. Make sure you play it to the rhythm of the song.

☐ Refer to the exercise above. Place your thumb on middle C and your second pointer finger on D.

☐ Play this exercise slowly. OPTIONAL: You can speed it up once you have mastered playing it slowly.

Here are some additional exercises to practice.

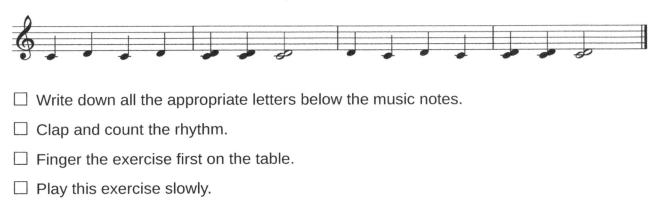

☐ Write down all the appropriate letters below the music notes.

☐ Clap and count the rhythm.

☐ Finger the exercise first on the table.

☐ Play this exercise slowly.

Video link: *https://www.musicmousestudios.com/piano-instructional-videos*

Additional Exercise 3

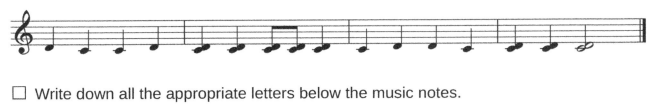

☐ Write down all the appropriate letters below the music notes.

☐ Clap and count the rhythm.

☐ Finger the exercise first on the table.

☐ Play this exercise slowly.

Video link: *https://www.musicmousestudios.com/piano-instructional-videos*

Congratulations, you've completed Lesson 2!

"To know how much there is to know is the beginning of learning to live."

—DOROTHY WEST

LESSON
3
Embarking on the Piano Adventure

Let's embark on a piano adventure together as we explore the foundations of proper hand and finger posture, new notes, music notation, and bring it all together in a delightful song! Let the musical journey begin!

Warmup Review

☐ Play all C's on the piano with your thumb.

☐ Play all D's on the piano with your 2nd finger.

No Sticky Fingers!

When playing the notes C-G in succession of each other, ensure that your fingers don't keep holding onto any of the previous notes you played. No "sticky fingers"! Focus on allowing each finger to play independently with a good, strong tone. Always practice slowly initially to ensure each finger plays evenly in speed and volume.

☐ Play the notes C through G five times with your right hand, fingers 1-5, respectively. Make sure you have the correct hand posture with the egg underneath, curved fingers, and no sticky fingers!

Video link*: https://www.musicmousestudios.com/piano-instructional-videos*

This week, we will focus on the new note E! E is played in your right hand with your middle or 3rd finger. On the treble clef staff, it is written on the bottom line.

This is where E is on the piano.

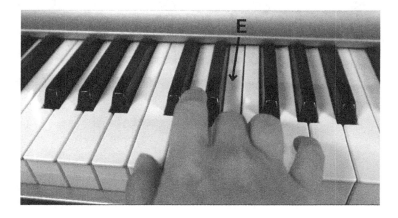

☐ Playing exercise: Find E on your piano.

Video link: *https://www.musicmousestudios.com/piano-instructional-videos*

Music Notation Exercise

☐ Draw a treble clef.

☐ Draw the notes C to G.

☐ Circle the note E.

Rhythm Exercise

☐ Review: Clap through the full rhythm tree.

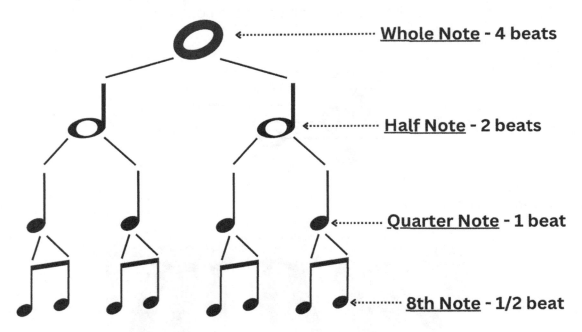

Whole Note - 4 beats

Half Note - 2 beats

Quarter Note - 1 beat

8th Note - 1/2 beat

C

☐ Look at the score above. Write down all the appropriate letters below the music notes.

In the last measure, when the notes are 3 letters apart (for example, C to D to E), this interval is called a **3rd**.

Answers

C　C　C　　D　D　D　　E　E　E　　C　E　C　E　CE　CE　CE

☐ Clap and count the rhythm in this exercise.

☐ Finger the song on the table to the rhythm you just clapped (C is played with your thumb, D is with your second finger, and E is with your third finger).

☐ Play this song slowly. OPTIONAL: You can speed it up once you have mastered it.

Video link: https://www.musicmousestudios.com/piano-instructional-videos

DAY 21-22 New Song: "Mary Had a Little Lamb"

We will play your first song – "Mary Had a Little Lamb!" Like the last lesson, remember to follow these steps before playing the music -

☐ Write down all the letters above the music notes.

☐ Clap and count the rhythm.

☐ Finger the exercise first on the table.

☐ Play this song slowly.

Video link: *https://www.musicmousestudios.com/piano-instructional-videos*

Mary Had a Little Lamb

Words by Sarah Josepha Hale
Traditional Melody

Ma - ry had a li - ttle lamb, li - ttle lamb, li - ttle lamb,

Ma - ry had a li - ttle lamb whose fleece was white as snow.

Check below to make sure you labeled the notes correctly!

Mary Had a Little Lamb

Words by Sarah Josepha Hale
Traditional Melody

E D C D E E E   D D D   E E E

E D C D E E E C D D E D C

About Sarah Josepha Hale

Born on October 24, 1788, in New Hampshire, Sarah was a renowned writer and editor. She was most well-known for her lyrics to "Mary Had a Little Lamb" and played a pivotal role in establishing Thanksgiving as a celebrated holiday. Some have revered her as the "Godmother of Thanksgiving" because, after the Civil War, she wrote to Abraham Lincoln, urging him to officially dedicate the last Thursday of November as a special day of gratitude to God for the blessings bestowed upon the nation. Lincoln thought this was a good idea and declared that all offices would be closed for National Thanksgiving Day on the last Thursday of November. This marked the beginning of what has become one of our most cherished and widely celebrated holidays annually.

Sarah's education consisted of being homeschooled by her mother and older brother, as well as a lot of self-learning. She went on to become a local school teacher and an acclaimed writer. Sarah was not only the first American *female* writer but the first novelist to tackle the topic of slavery. *Northwood: Life North and South*, published in 1827, was a huge success. In it, Sarah recommended relocating slaves from America to Liberia. She stated that slavery was not only harmful and dehumanizing to the slaves but also to their owners, stunting them both morally and psychologically.

In 1830, she wrote *Poems for Our Children*, which contains *"Mary Had a Little Lamb"* (originally *"Mary's Lamb")*.

☐ Play through "Mary Had a Little Lamb" again.

Controversy About the Origins of "Mary Had a Little Lamb"

This nursery song was allegedly based on an actual girl named Mary, who, in 1815, was assisting her father on the farm when she found a sick newborn lamb. She pleaded with her dad to keep it. Against all odds, Mary nursed the lamb back to health. This lamb followed Mary everywhere she went and indeed had "fleece white as snow." Mary even took the lamb to school one day and hid the lamb beneath her desk under a blanket. When the teacher called her to the front of the class to answer a question, the lamb ran up to follow her. The teacher quickly shooed the lamb out. One of her older classmates, John Roulstone, wrote a poem about what had happened to her that day at school and handed it to Mary. Here was his poem:

> *Mary had a little lamb;*
> *Its fleece was white as snow;*
> *And everywhere that Mary went,*
> *The lamb was sure to go.*
>
> *It followed her to school one day,*
> *Which was against the rule;*
> *It made the children laugh and play*
> *To see a lamb at school.*
>
> *And so the teacher turned it out;*
> *But still it lingered near,*
> *And waited patiently about*
> *Till Mary did appear.*

Hale's version contained 3 additional stanzas, and Mary said she didn't know how Hale obtained her poem. Hale claims to have made up *Mary's Lamb.* In the 1920s, after both Mary Sawyer and Sarah Hale had died, Henry Ford, the founder of Ford Motor Company, bought Mary's old schoolhouse and published a book about Mary Sawyer and her lamb!

☐ Perform "Mary Had a Little Lamb" for someone or share it with us on our website, music-mousestudios.com!

Congratulations, you've completed Lesson 3!

"I never dreamed about
success. I worked for it."

—ESTÉE LAUDER

LESSON
4
Getting in the Groove

In this lesson, we will be focusing on some new notes as
well as some groovin' new rhythms! Get ready!!

Warmup Review

☐ Play all C's on the piano with your thumb.

☐ Play all D's on the piano with your 2nd finger.

☐ Play all E's on the piano with your 3rd finger.

☐ Play ascending C D E F G and then descending G F E D C with your right hand.

Repeat this five times. Ensure you have the correct hand posture with the egg underneath, curved fingers, and no sticky fingers!

Video link: *https://www.musicmousestudios.com/piano-instructional-videos*

New Note F

This week, we are highlighting the new note F! F is played in your right hand with your ring or 4th finger. On the staff, it is written on the bottom space.

This is where F is on the piano.

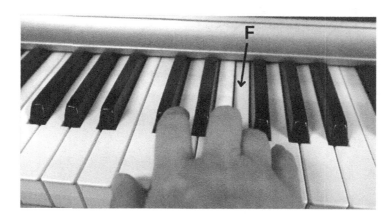

☐ Playing exercise: Find F on your piano.

Video link: https://www.musicmousestudios.com/piano-instructional-videos

Music Notation Exercise

☐ Draw a treble clef.

☐ Draw the notes C to G.

☐ Circle the note F.

Rhythm Exercise

☐ Review: Clap through the full rhythm tree.

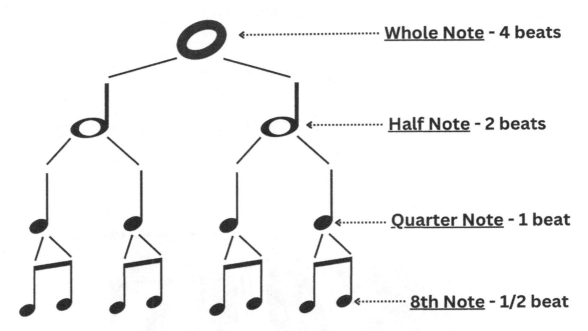

Whole Note - 4 beats

Half Note - 2 beats

Quarter Note - 1 beat

8th Note - 1/2 beat

☐ Look at the score above. Write down all the appropriate letters below the music notes.

Answers below:

C C C C   D D D D D   E E E E   F F F F   C C F F F   CF CF CF

In the last measure, when the notes are 4 letters apart from each other (C to D to E to F), this interval is called a **4th**.

☐ Clap and count the rhythm. It should sound like the following.

   Video link: *https://www.musicmousestudios.com/piano-instructional-videos*

☐ Finger the song on the table to the rhythm you just clapped (C is played with your thumb, D is with your second finger, E is with your third finger, and F is with your fourth finger).

☐ Play this exercise slowly. OPTIONAL: You can speed it up once you have mastered it.

Music Theory

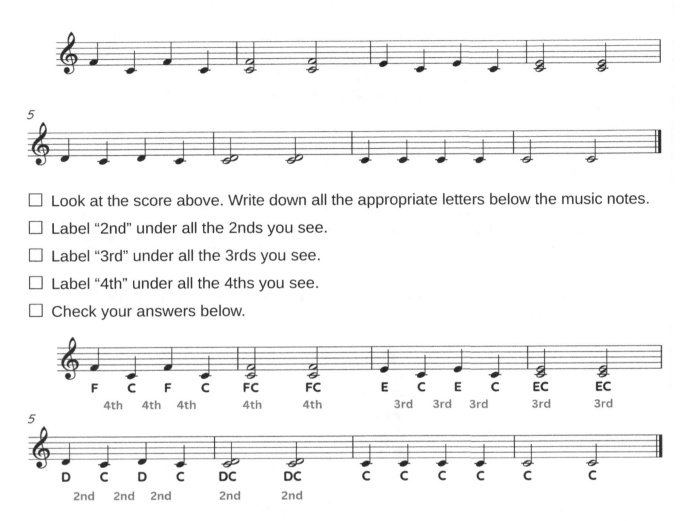

☐ Look at the score above. Write down all the appropriate letters below the music notes.

☐ Label "2nd" under all the 2nds you see.

☐ Label "3rd" under all the 3rds you see.

☐ Label "4th" under all the 4ths you see.

☐ Check your answers below.

☐ Clap and count the rhythm. It should sound like the following.

Video link: https://www.musicmousestudios.com/piano-instructional-videos

Playing Exercise

☐ Finger the song on the table to the rhythm you clapped in the last exercise (C is played with your thumb, D is with your second finger, E is with your third finger, and F is with your fourth finger).

☐ Play this exercise slowly. OPTIONAL: You can speed it up once you have mastered it.

Video link: https://www.musicmousestudios.com/piano-instructional-videos

Dotted Quarter Notes

A dotted quarter note is 1.5 beats. This means it's faster than a quarter note but slower than a half note.

In our rhythm tree, we learned that a quarter note consists of two 8th notes. On the other hand, a dotted quarter note is made up of three 8th notes.

Dotted quarter notes look just like quarter notes but have a dot at the end.

How do we count dotted quarter notes? We count it as "1&2." Think about how you clap a quarter note ("1&") and add another 8th note to it ("2"). Because a dotted quarter note is 1.5 beats, we count one full beat with "1&" and then half a beat with the "2." Refer to the picture below to see how a dotted quarter followed by an 8th note is notated.

The rhythm you are playing for a dotted quarter note is the same as a quarter note plus an 8th note.

***Video link**: https://www.musicmousestudios.com/piano-instructional-videos*

New Song: "Down the River"

Down the River

Andrea Chang

5

☐ Look at the score above. Write down all the letters below the music notes. What patterns do you see?

☐ Label all the melodic 2nds, 3rds, and 4ths in the song.

☐ Clap and count the rhythm. It should sound like the following -

Video link*: https://www.musicmousestudios.com/piano-instructional-videos*

☐ Finger the song on the table to the rhythm you just clapped (C is played with your thumb, D is with your second finger, E is with your third finger, and F is with your fourth finger).

☐ Play this song slowly. OPTIONAL: You can speed it up once you have mastered it.

About Andrea Chang

Andrea is the author of this book and is a veteran in both the audio and video games/tech industry, where she has worked for over a decade. Her experience at Hi-Rez Studios, a video game company, where she has served both as an Audio Director and an Executive Producer. She built the audio team there from the ground up and has also supervised the centralized audio, art, production and outsourcing teams. Andrea has also provided high-level audio direction as well as hands-on audio support, for all things related to music, sound design, and VO, for all the games and cinematics at Hi-Rez, such as Rogue Company, Smite,

Paladins, Realm Royale, Divine Knockout, and other unannounced games.

Andrea has also worked at Microsoft as an Audio Lead on the HoloLens App, "Actiongram," featuring collaborations with George Takei, Warcraft, Hello Kitty, etc., as well as working as a Senior Sound Designer on the Central Audio Team, supporting audio for company-wide HoloLens and Windows experiences. She sound designed, composed music, implemented audio for augmented and virtual reality across various platforms and devices such as the HoloLens, and VR headsets, among others, and designed audio prototypes to drive innovation across the organization.

In addition, Andrea has also worked at Electronic Arts (EA) as an in-house sound designer on their eSports Multiplayer Online Battle Arena game, "Dawngate," as well as having freelanced in the video game and film industry. For a sample of her work, visit www.musicmousestudios.com.

Since covid-19 started, Andrea has homeschooled her daughter. She has detailed her learnings, tips, and tricks on successfully juggling working and homeschooling in her book, *A Working Mom's Guide: How to Homeschool Without Losing Your Mind*.

As a content creator, she also enjoys regularly uploading free piano and education resources on her YouTube Channel @homeschoolingwithandrea as well as creating music covers with her daughter. She founded Music Mouse Studios to provide educational and music resources for both kids and adults to help them achieve their dreams.

COVER

☐ Perform "Down the River" for someone or share it with us on our website, www.music-mousestuios.com!

Congratulations, you've completed Lesson 4!

"Develop success from failures.
Discouragement and failure are two of
the surest stepping stones to success."

—DALE CARNEGIE

LESSON
5
Discovering the Joy

In this lesson, we will be expanding our skillset and learning how to play a famous song called "Ode to Joy" by a well-known composer – Ludwig van Beethoven!

☐ Play all the C's on the piano with your thumb.

☐ Play all the D's on the piano with your 2nd finger.

☐ Play all the E's on the piano with your 3rd finger.

☐ Play all the F's on the piano with your 4th finger.

☐ Play the notes C D E F G ascending and then G F E D C descending with your right hand. Repeat this five times. Make sure you have the correct hand posture with the egg underneath, curved fingers, and no sticky fingers!

This week, we will focus on the new note G! G is played in your right hand with your pinky or 5th finger. On the treble clef staff, it is written on the second line.

This is where G is on the piano.

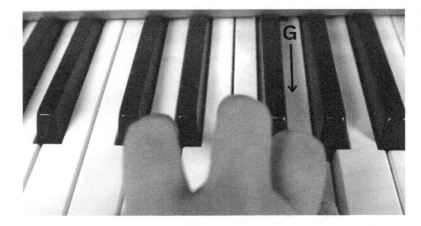

☐ Playing exercise: Find G on your piano.

Video link: *https://www.musicmousestudios.com/piano-instructional-videos*

Music Notation Exercise

☐ Draw a treble clef.

☐ Draw the notes middle C, D, E, F, and G.

☐ Circle the note G.

Rhythm Exercises

☐ Review: Clap through the full rhythm tree.

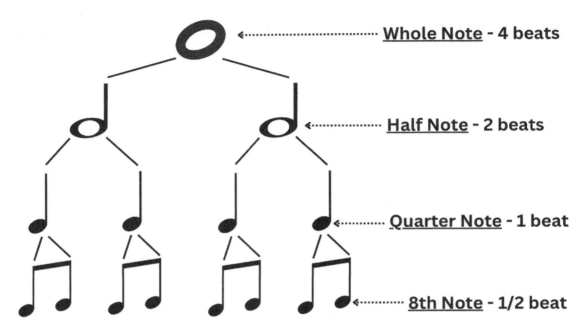

Whole Note - 4 beats

Half Note - 2 beats

Quarter Note - 1 beat

8th Note - 1/2 beat

☐ Practice clapping the rhythm below.

1 & 2 & 3 & 4 &   1 & 2 & 3 & 4 &   1 & 2 & 3 & 4 &   1 & 2 & 3 & 4 &

☐ Look at the score. Write down all the letters below the music notes. The answers are below.

In the last measure, when the notes are 5 letters apart from each other in those chords (i.e., from C to D to E to F to G), this interval is called a **5th**.

Answer

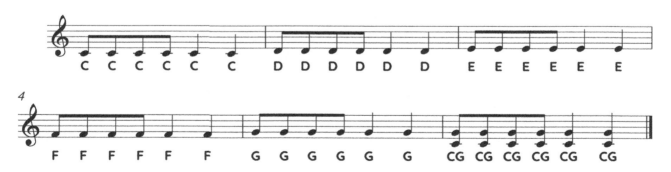

☐ Clap and count the rhythm. It should sound like the following.

   Video link*: https://www.musicmousestudios.com/piano-instructional-videos*

☐ Finger the song on the table to the rhythm you just clapped (C is played with your thumb, D is with your second finger, E is with your third finger, F is with your fourth finger, G is with your fifth finger).

☐ Play this exercise slowly. OPTIONAL: You can speed it up once you have mastered it.

Playing Exercise 2

☐ Find D on the piano.

☐ Play a 5th up starting from D.

☐ Find E on the piano.

☐ Play a 5th up starting from E.

☐ Find F on the piano.

☐ Play a 5th up starting from F.

☐ Find G on the piano.

☐ Play a 5th up starting from G.

☐ Practice playing 5ths beginning on any note on the piano.

Video link: https://www.musicmousestudios.com/piano-instructional-videos

DAY 43-46 New Song: "Ode to Joy"

Ode to Joy

Ludwig van Beethoven

Joy - ful, joy - ful, we a - dore Thee, God of glo - ry, Lord of love;

Hearts un - fold like flow'rs be - fore Thee, Op' - ning to the sun a - bove.

☐ Write down all the letters below the music notes in this song.

☐ What patterns do you see? Do the first and second rows of music look similar?

☐ Clap and count the rhythm. It should sound like the following.

Video link: https://www.musicmousestudios.com/piano-instructional-videos

☐ Finger the song on the table to the rhythm you just clapped (C is played with your thumb, D is with your second finger, E is with your third finger, F is with your fourth finger, G is with your fifth finger). Pay special attention to the last measure in each row with a dotted quarter note rhythm. Make sure you feel confident playing the last measure of each row before playing it on the piano.

☐ Play this song slowly. OPTIONAL: You can speed it up once you have mastered it.

About Ludwig van Beethoven

Ludwig van Beethoven, one of the most well-known composers of all time, was born on December 17, 1770, and lived until March 26, 1827. Hailing from Germany, he was a prolific composer despite the profound challenge of losing his hearing at the age of 28. Over the course of 45 remarkable years, Beethoven crafted a colossal body of work, encompassing 722 compositions. Among his magnificent portfolio are 35 piano sonatas, 16 string quartets, 9 symphonies, and a single opera, each a testament to his genius.

In Beethoven's early years, his musical education began under the stern tutelage of his father. Escaping a tumultuous family life plagued by his father's descent into alcoholism, Beethoven found solace with the family of Helene von Breuning. Helene, who he considered his "second mother," educated him and introduced him to the upper social circles. He loved this family and taught their children piano. He also taught piano to the Brunswick family, where he developed intimate connections with the sisters Therese and Josephine Brunsvik. Beethoven harbored an enduring passion for Josephine, but societal constraints prevented their union. Eventually, he encountered Josephine's cousin, Julie "Giulietta" Guicciardi, with whom he had a fervent infatuation as well, which inspired him to compose the renowned "Moonlight Sonata" (Piano Sonata No. 14) in her honor.

In 1784, Beethoven briefly studied with Mozart in Vienna, leaving a memorable impression on the renowned maestro, who declared, "This young man will make a great name for himself in the world." The esteemed composer Haydn, who had mentored Mozart, offered to teach and mentor Beethoven when the prodigy reached the age of 21. Beethoven deeply admired George Frideric Handel and regarded him as "the greatest composer who ever lived."

The year 1814 marked a pivotal moment in Beethoven's life as his hearing loss intensified, ultimately compelling him to retire from performing in public. In a poignant series of letters to his brother, known as the Heiligenstadt Testament, penned in 1802, Beethoven divulged his struggles with deteriorating health and the profound personal loneliness he endured. Despite his seclusion and complete deafness, in this final decade of his life, Beethoven crafted some of his most cherished and revered works, including late piano sonatas, string quartets, and his magnum opus, Symphony No.

9. Notably, the rousing "Ode to Joy" (the song we learned), was a climactic moment within Symphony No. 9, debuted with Beethoven himself conducting completely deaf. He was entirely unaware of the thunderous ovation from the audience cheering behind him until one of the musicians alerted him to the overwhelming response.

Beethoven's life, marked by triumph over adversity and an unwavering dedication to his craft, continues to inspire generations with the enduring power of his music.

☐ Perform "Ode to Joy" for someone or share with us on our website, www.musicmouse-studios.com!

Congratulations, you've completed Lesson 5!

"When we strive to become better than we are, everything around us becomes better too."

—PAULO COELHO

LESSON
6
Silence is Golden

In this lesson, we will shift our focus to the significance of silence in music – discover how sometimes the power lies in what we don't play!

☐ Play ascending C D E F G and then descending G F E D C with your right hand. Repeat this five times. Make sure you have the correct hand posture with the egg underneath, curved fingers, and no sticky fingers!

Rests are moments in music when you don't play anything and remain silent. Similar to notes in the rhythm tree, there are also different types of rests as well. Quarter rests, like quarter notes, are 1 beat of silence. Equivalently, half rests are 2 beats of silence, and 8th rests are half a beat of silence. A half rest looks like a hat; conversely, a whole rest looks like an upside-down hat. A quarter rest looks like a squiggly "3," while an 8th rest looks like a little fancy "7."

Take a look at the rests tree below and familiarize yourself with it.

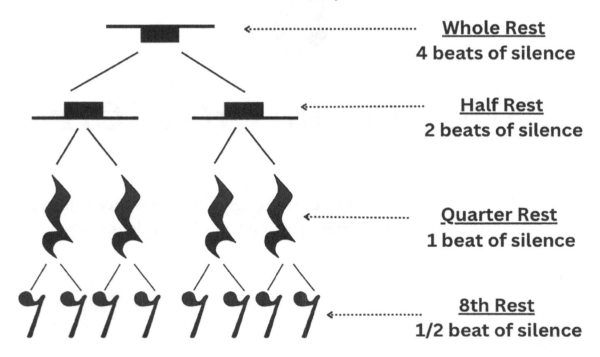

Whole Rest
4 beats of silence

Half Rest
2 beats of silence

Quarter Rest
1 beat of silence

8th Rest
1/2 beat of silence

Video link: https://www.musicmousestudios.com/piano-instructional-videos

Music Notation

A whole rest, half rest, quarter rest, and 8th rest are respectively seen above. On the staff, counting from the bottom line up, the whole rest hangs below the 4th line. The half rest sits on top of the 3rd line, while the quarter rest is between the staff's bottom and top lines. The 8th rests are smaller, so they sit between the 2nd and 4th lines of the staff.

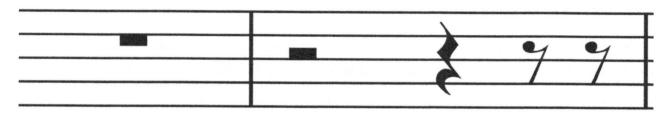

Music Notation Exercise

☐ Use the staff above to draw a whole rest.

☐ Use the staff above to draw a half rest.

☐ Use the staff above to draw a quarter rest.

☐ Use the staff above to draw an eighth rest.

Half Rests Exercises

Let's take a look at some half rests exercises. Clap the exercises below. Remember that on the rests, you don't clap (for example, in Exercise 1, don't clap on beats 3 and 4).

Video link: https://www.musicmousestudios.com/piano-instructional-videos

Exercise 1

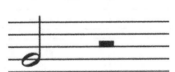

Exercise 2

Exercise 3

Exercise 4

Can you play all 4 Half Rests Exercises together? Give it a try slowly!

Quarter Rests Exercises

Let's take a look at some quarter rests exercises. Clap Exercise 1 below – remember that on the rests, you don't clap (for example, in Exercise 1, don't clap on beats 2 and 4).

Video link: https://www.musicmousestudios.com/piano-instructional-videos

Exercise 1

Exercise 2

Exercise 3

1   2   3   4

Exercise 4

Can you play all 4 Quarter Rest Exercises together? Try it out!

8th Rests Exercises

Let's take a look at some 8th rests exercises. Clap Exercise 1 below – remember that on the rests, you don't clap (for example, in Exercise 1, don't clap on the &'s of every beat).

Video link: https://www.musicmousestudios.com/piano-instructional-videos

Exercise 1

Exercise 2

Exercise 3

Exercise 4

Can you play all four 8th Rest Exercises together? You can do it! 😊

Whole Rests Exercises

Whole rests are straightforward – you don't play anything for 4 beats! Give it a try below.

DAY 53 — $\frac{4}{4}$ Time Signature

At the beginning of every staff, we have a clef and then a time signature. A time signature tells us how many beats are in a measure and the unit of measurement for a beat. In 4/4, the top 4 tells us that there are 4 beats in a measure, and the bottom 4 tells us that the quarter note gets 1 beat. All of the songs we have played this far have been in 4/4, but later pieces will have other time signatures, which not only will have different numbers in them, but the music will also have a different feel. In 4/4, beats 1 and 3 will feel stronger, and beats 2 and 4 will feel weaker.

 # beats per measure
There are 4 beats per a measure
What note gets 1 beat?
When 4's on the bottom, quarter gets 1 beat

Fill in the Beats!

☐ To complete each measure, draw the missing rhythm note(s) on the note G.

☐ Check your answers below.

☐ Draw the missing rhythm note(s) on the note G.

☐ Check your answers below.

New Song: "Oh When the Saints Go Marching In"

Oh When the Saints Go Marching In

Traditional

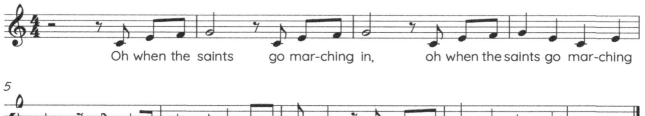

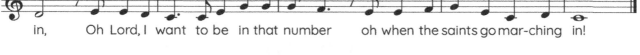

☐ Write down all the letters for "Oh When the Saints Go Marching In."

☐ Clap and count the rhythm. It should sound like the following -

Video link: *https://www.musicmousestudios.com/piano-instructional-videos*

Pay special attention to measure 7, which has a rhythm that's a bit trickier. You might want to practice clapping this measure individually a couple of times first.

☐ Finger the song on the table to the rhythm you just clapped (C is played with your thumb, D is with your second finger, E is with your third finger, F is with your fourth finger, G is with your fifth finger).

☐ Play this song slowly. OPTIONAL: You can speed it up once you have mastered it.

Congratulations, you've completed Lesson 6!

"Opportunity is missed by most people because it is dressed in overalls and looks like work."

—THOMAS EDISON

LESSON
7
Milky Way Melodies

In this lesson, we will be learning a beloved and recognizable song. Get ready to embark on a musical journey that will bring the celestial wonders to life at your fingertips!

☐ Play ascending C D E F G and then descending G F E D C with your right hand. Repeat this five times. Make sure you have the correct hand posture with the egg underneath, curved fingers, and no sticky fingers!

☐ Find middle C with your left hand. Go to the C below this with your pinky in your left hand. Now place your 4th finger on this D (below middle C), 3rd finger on this E (below middle C), 2nd finger on F (below middle C), and thumb on G (below middle C). These are the same notes (C D E F G) but with your left hand.

☐ Play C D E F G (all these notes below middle C) ascending and descending with your left hand 5 times. Practice slowly to ensure no sticky fingers!

This week, we will focus on the new note A! A is the note next to G. On the staff, it is written in the second space.

This is where A is on the piano.

☐ Playing exercise: Find A on your piano.

Video link: https://www.musicmousestudios.com/piano-instructional-videos

Music Notation Exercise

☐ Draw a treble clef followed by the notes C, D, E, F, G, and A

☐ Circle A.

Metronome

A metronome is a device that plays a constant beat and helps you play and practice music at a consistent tempo. **Tempo** refers to the speed at which you play a song. Sometimes when you're practicing, you may accidentally play at an uneven speed (for example, with a row of 8th notes, you may play the first and second ones fast but the last two slower because you're stumbling on the notes). Practicing with a metronome helps to ensure that you follow the beat and play every note in each respective rhythm evenly in speed.

There are various types of metronomes. Some are analog, and some are digital. Others you can download as an app on your phone. If you type "Metronome" in your App Store, you should be able to find metronome apps that are either free or very cheap. With each metronome, you can drag up or down the lever to raise or lower the number, which reflects the tempo or the BPM (beats per minute). A higher number indicates a faster tempo, while a lower number indicates a slower tempo.

If you happen to "fall off" the metronome train and either get behind or ahead of the beat, you can pause for a second and wait for the next beat to play the correct note in time. When practicing a new song, always put the metronome at a slow tempo (quarter note = 50 or lower is a good starting point) and practice at that speed until you can play every single note correctly. Only then should you gradually raise the tempo upon subsequent playthroughs of the music.

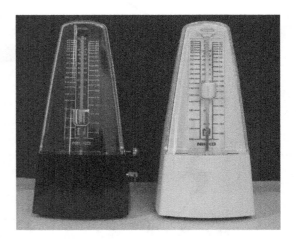

☐ Get a metronome – either buy one or download a metronome app on your phone (often, they are free).

Rhythm Exercise

☐ Set your metronome to 60 bpm. Follow the metronome's beat and clap through the full rhythm tree at this tempo.

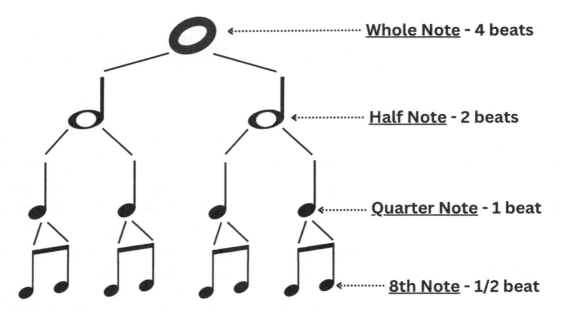

Whole Note - 4 beats

Half Note - 2 beats

Quarter Note - 1 beat

8th Note - 1/2 beat

☐ With your metronome still at 60 bpm, use your hands to silently "clap" through the full rests tree. Put both hands to the side every time you have to indicate a beat is passing.

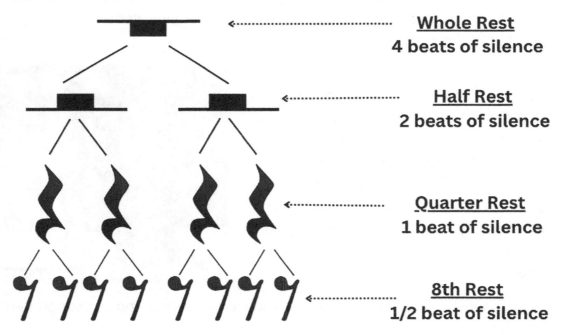

Whole Rest
4 beats of silence

Half Rest
2 beats of silence

Quarter Rest
1 beat of silence

8th Rest
1/2 beat of silence

Twinkle Twinkle Little Star

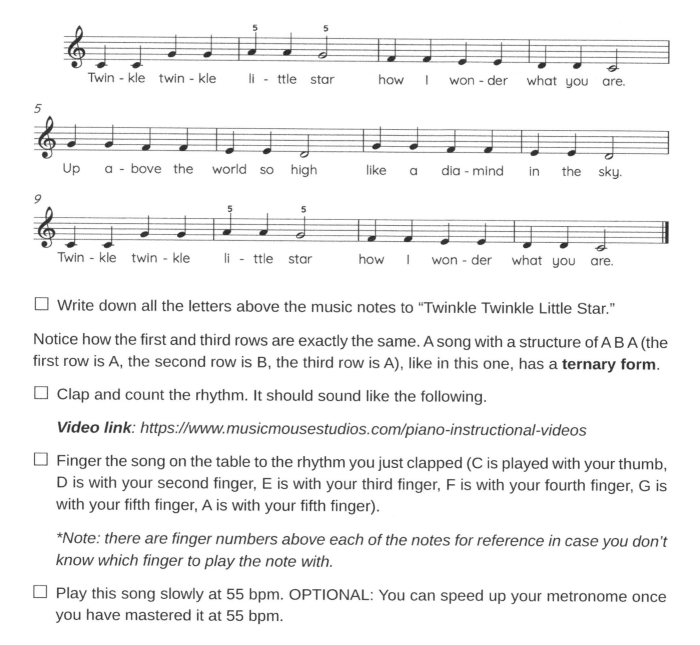

☐ Write down all the letters above the music notes to "Twinkle Twinkle Little Star."

Notice how the first and third rows are exactly the same. A song with a structure of A B A (the first row is A, the second row is B, the third row is A), like in this one, has a **ternary form**.

☐ Clap and count the rhythm. It should sound like the following.

Video link: https://www.musicmousestudios.com/piano-instructional-videos

☐ Finger the song on the table to the rhythm you just clapped (C is played with your thumb, D is with your second finger, E is with your third finger, F is with your fourth finger, G is with your fifth finger, A is with your fifth finger).

Note: there are finger numbers above each of the notes for reference in case you don't know which finger to play the note with.

☐ Play this song slowly at 55 bpm. OPTIONAL: You can speed up your metronome once you have mastered it at 55 bpm.

DAY 64

About Jane Taylor

Jane Taylor was a poet who lived from 1783 to 1824 in England. She is most widely known for having written the lyrics to "Twinkle Twinkle Little Star." She comes from a literary family – her sister was also a poet, her dad was an engraver, and her mom was a writer. Jane and her sister Ann published various poetry collections together, such as the successful *Original Poems for Infant Minds*, *Rhymes for Nursery* and *Hymns for Infant Minds*. She, unfortunately, died at the age of 40 of breast cancer.

We will now add some of the intervals we previously learned to "Twinkle Twinkle Little Star" to make it even more amazing!

☐ Look at the score below. Write down all the letters above the music notes. Notice how the first and the third rows are the same. Once again, we see that the song has a **ternary form**.

The Amazing Twinkle Twinkle Little Star

Arr. by Andrea Chang

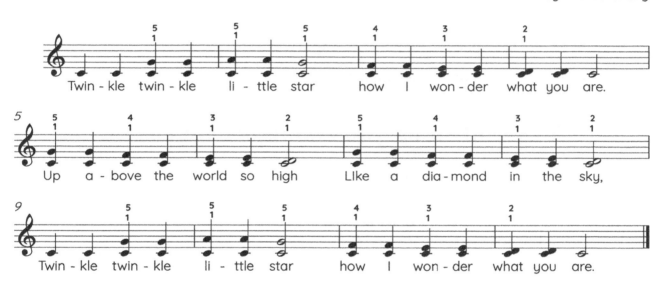

☐ Clap and count the rhythm. It should sound like the following.

Video link: https://www.musicmousestudios.com/piano-instructional-videos

☐ Finger the song on the table to the rhythm you just clapped (C is played with your thumb, D is with your second finger, E is with your third finger, F is with your fourth finger, G is with your fifth finger, A is with your fifth finger). Be sure to play all chords with the correct fingering.

Note: there are finger numbers above each of the notes for reference in case you don't know which finger to play the note with.

☐ Play this song slowly at 55 bpm. OPTIONAL: You can speed up your metronome once you have mastered it at 55 bpm.

In the second measure, when the notes are 6 letters apart from each other (for example, C to D to E to F to G to A), this interval is called a **6th**.

☐ Circle all the 6ths that you see in this song.

☐ Point to all the 5ths that you see in this song.

☐ Point to all the 4ths that you see in this song.

☐ Point to all the 3rds that you see in this song.

☐ Point to all the 2nds that you see in this song.

Congratulations, you've completed Lesson 7!

"When you have a dream, you've got to grab it and never let go."

—CAROL BURNETT

LESSON
8
The Memory Maze

But how do you remember what all of the notes are?! In this lesson,
we will go over tips and tricks on how to navigate this memory maze!

Introducing… the C Major Scale

What is a **scale**? The English alphabet has 26 letters. The musical alphabet has 7 letters, and these form a scale. In C Major, this scale consists of all the white notes on the piano – C, D, E, F, G, A, B. After B, it returns to C again, and the pattern continues until you run out of keys on the piano!

This week we will learn how to play an ascending C Major scale with our right hand!

To finger a C Major scale with your right hand, play the following notes with these fingers in this order:

Ascending

C – Finger 1

D – Finger 2

E – Finger 3

F – Finger 1 – you will cross your thumb underneath your third finger, which is on E, and place your thumb on F

G – Finger 2

A – Finger 3

B – Finger 4

C – Finger 5

This is what your finger should look like going from E to F with the thumb crossing under.

Today we are only focusing on ascending. We will practice descending in another lesson.

Watch this video to see it in action -

Video link: *https://www.musicmousestudios.com/piano-instructional-videos*

Warmup

☐ Play an ascending C Major Scale with your right hand 5 times, starting at middle C.

☐ With your left hand, play C D E F G (all these notes below middle C) ascending and then G F E D C descending all together 5 times. Practice slowly to ensure no sticky fingers!

C Major Scale Notation

This is what an ascending C Major Scale looks like written out on the treble clef staff.

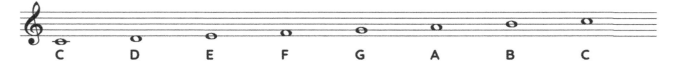

DAY 69 New Note B

Our new note today is B! B is next to A. In the treble clef, it is written on the third line.

This is where B is on the piano.

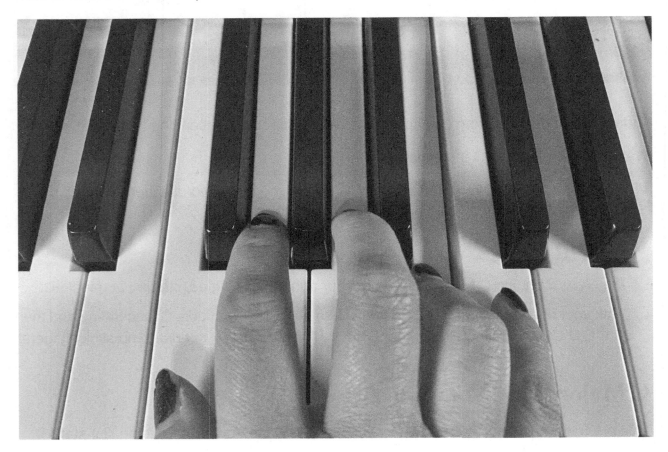

☐ Playing exercise: Find B on your piano and play it with your fourth finger in your right hand.

When the notes in the chord are 7 letters apart, this interval is called a **7th**. For example, C to B is a 7th because there are 7 letters from C (1) to D (2) to E (3) to F (4) to G (5) to A (6) to B (7).

☐ Playing exercise: Find middle C on the piano and then play the B you learned simultaneously. You will want to play C with your thumb and B with your pinky. It should look like the picture below.

Notes Above B

Now that you know the notes C, D, E, F, G, A, and B, the notes beyond B will keep repeating themselves with that pattern again, starting at C, up and down the piano for a C Major scale.

Regarding notation, if you continue to go up each space and line note, the written notes also keep repeating themselves. Every time the notes repeat themselves, we call this an **octave**. An octave is also an interval, similar to the 7th we just learned. An octave occurs when there are 8 steps in between the two notes. In our case, it is from middle C to the octave above middle C. Octaves, like the other intervals we've been learning, can be written harmonically (as a chord) or melodically (sequentially), as seen in the picture below.

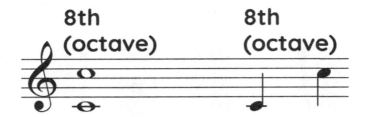

This is what it looks like on the piano – place your right thumb on middle C and your right pinky on the C above middle C. It is one key over to the right from playing a 7th.

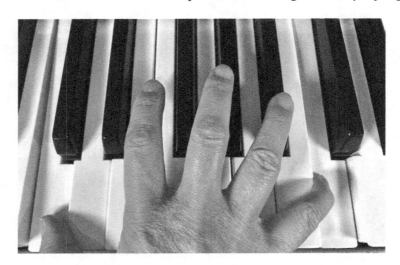

☐ Playing exercise #1: Play an octave with your right thumb on middle C and your right pinky on the C above middle C *at the same time.* This is a **harmonic octave.**

☐ Playing exercise #2: Now play middle C with your thumb, and then play the C above middle C with your pinky *after* that. This is a **melodic octave** because it is **arpeggiated**.

Extended Notes of the Scale

Look at the picture below to see what the notes of C Major (extended two octaves above middle C) on a treble clef look like on the staff.

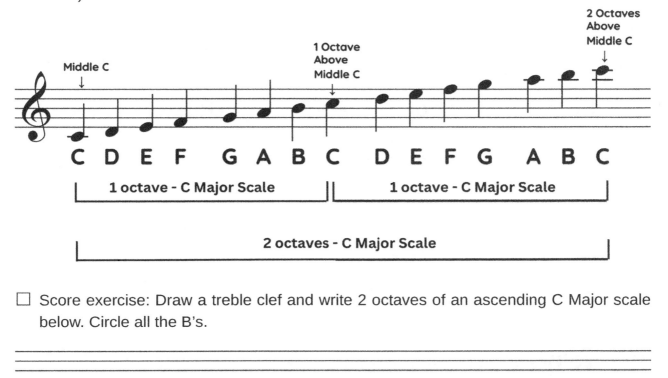

☐ Score exercise: Draw a treble clef and write 2 octaves of an ascending C Major scale below. Circle all the B's.

A full piano has 88 keys, consisting of 7 octaves and three lower notes below that (B, B flat, and A).

☐ Look at the graphic below and label all the notes on this 88 keys piano.

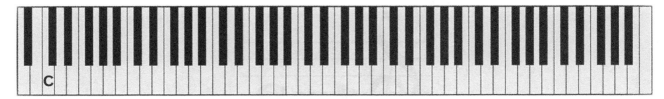

Now that you know what C, D, E, F, G, A, and B look like on the piano, it's time to memorize what they look like on the staff. Aside from remembering which space and line note goes with which letter notes, there are a couple of acronyms tricks that can help, which we will discuss in the next lesson!

Notes Acronyms: Unlocking Memorization Tips

A simple way to memorize the **line** notes on the staff (E G B D F) in the treble clef is the following acronym "**E**very **G**ood **B**oy **D**oes **F**ine."

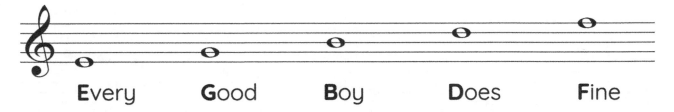

| **Every** | **Good** | **Boy** | **Does** | **Fine** |

A simple way to memorize the **space** notes on the staff in the treble clef (F A C E) is that it spells the word "**face.**"

| **F** | **A** | **C** | **E** |

The "G Trick": Unlocking Memorization Tips

If all else fails and you still can't remember all of the notes, an easier way to figure out what the notes are in a treble clef is to remember that the treble clef is also known as the "G Clef." This is because where the treble clef curves inward is where the note G is located on the staff. Knowing where G is, you can count up or down on the staff to figure out the note in question.

Name that Note!

Let's practice! Feel free to use any of the above methods to determine the notes.

☐ Write down the letter name under each note below.

Answers

G D B F A E C C G E D F C A B

New Song: "Go Tell Aunt Rhody"

Take a look at this song, "Go Tell Aunt Rhody," below. Observe how it consists of three distinct sections – Part A, Part B, and a return to Part A again. It's helpful to distinguish the underlying structure of a song, as it identifies any recurring sections to save on practice time. Notice how it is broken apart into 3 sections – Part A, Part B, and then Part A again. Like "Twinkle, Twinkle Little Star," this song is in **ternary form**. On Day 73, practice Part A; on Day 74, practice Part B; on Day 75, practice Part A and putting it all together; on Day 76, solidify putting Part A, B, and A together and try to perform it for someone!

A note about fingering: fingering may change depending on what notes are in the song and how far you have to stretch your fingers in between notes. We may not always, for example, play C with our thumbs, D with our index fingers, E with our third fingers, etc. The fingering below is the smoothest route for your fingers to move quickly from one note to another for this particular song.

☐ Write down all the letters below the music notes for "Go Tell Aunt Rhody."

☐ Clap and count the rhythm. It should sound like the following.

   Video link: https://www.musicmousestudios.com/piano-instructional-videos

☐ Finger the song on the table to the rhythm you just clapped. *Follow the finger numbers listed above each of the notes.*

☐ Play this song slowly at 55 bpm. OPTIONAL: You can speed up your metronome once you have mastered it at 55 bpm.

Go Tell Aunt Rhody

Jean-Jacques Rousseau

About Jean-Jacques Rousseau

Jean-Jacques Rousseau, the composer of "Go Tell Aunt Rhody," lived from 1712 to 1778 and was born in Geneva. He was regarded as a philosopher, writer, and composer. His *Discourse on Inequality* and *The Social Contract* played an instrumental role in shaping the tenets of the Age of Enlightenment as well as parts of the French Revolution in regard to the economy, politics, and education.

Within *The Social Contract*, Rousseau proclaims, "Man is born free, and everywhere he is in chains. Those who think themselves the masters of others are indeed greater slaves than they." He believed that the establishment of various forms of government, be it monarchy, aristocracy, or democracy, stemmed from inequalities in society, which would inevitably spark new revolutions aimed at toppling existing systems, only to find that the new leaders would perpetuate and exacerbate the very disparities they sought to rectify. Nevertheless, Rousseau was convinced that humanity possessed an innate desire for progress, which would create improved political systems that genuinely served the collective welfare.

As a composer, Rousseau's music was a fusion of Baroque and Classical styles. Much like his philosophical pursuits, the concept of freedom is a pillar in many of his musical works. There is an emphasis on the melody, which laid the foundation for the Romantic period, where expression eclipsed the rigid constraints and methodologies of the Baroque and Classical eras. Rousseau composed seven operas, drawing recognition from luminaries such as Mozart and Beethoven. Beethoven himself crafted a standalone song from Rousseau's one-act opera "The Village Soothsayer" and titled it "Non, Colette n'est point trompeuse." It is within this same opera that the melody for "Go Tell Aunt Rhody" comes from.

Congratulations, you've completed Lesson 8!

"Believe you can and you're halfway there."

—THEODORE ROOSEVELT

LESSON
9
Dual Hand Artistry

The spotlight now shines on the left hand! This lesson is dedicated to all the left-handed players as we explore the art of incorporating the left alongside the right hand for a harmonious union of musical expression.

Descending C Major Scale
Right Hand

But first, let's finish out our C Major scale with our right hand. A descending C Major Scale with your right hand is the same as ascending except in reverse order. See below for the fingering.

Descending

C (above middle C) – Finger 5

B (above middle C) – Finger 4

A (above middle C) – Finger 3

G (above middle C) – Finger 2

F (above middle C) – Finger 1

E (above middle C) – Finger 3 – your 3rd finger will cross over your thumb

D (above middle C) – Finger 2

C (middle C) – Finger 1

In the figure below, the fingering will start on the right side and go toward the left.

The main place to pay attention to is going from F back down to E and crossing that **3rd** finger over your thumb, as seen in the picture below.

Video link: *https://www.musicmousestudios.com/piano-instructional-videos*

Warmup – Review

☐ Practice playing a descending C Major scale with your right hand 5 times, starting at the C above middle C.

☐ Play an ascending and descending C Major scale with your right hand 5 times.

☐ With your left hand, play C D E F G (all these notes below middle C) ascending and then descending G F E D C 5 times. Practice slowly to ensure no sticky fingers!

DAY 79

New Note C in Bass Clef

Middle C is the same note we played on the piano with our right hand, but this time we will play it with our left hand.

☐ Playing exercise #1: Find middle C and then play it with your left thumb.

☐ Playing exercise #2: Now find the C below that. Play this lower C with your pinky. This is the same C you've been playing in your warm-ups with your left hand.

This is what the notes look like on the staff. Notice how these two C's make an **octave**. Similar to our lesson with right hand octaves, the left hand can also be written as broken or arpeggiated melodic octaves or stacked together like a chord for harmonic octaves.

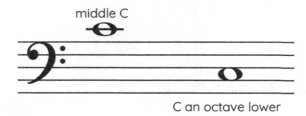

middle C

C an octave lower

Playing Octaves

You can play octaves on any note, with any hand. Generally, when playing octaves, you will play with your thumb and pinky so that your hand can stretch across all the notes more easily. In your left hand, the pinky is on the bottom note of the octave, and the thumb is on the top note of the octave. In your right hand, it's the opposite, with your thumb on the bottom note of the octave and your pinky on the top note of the octave.

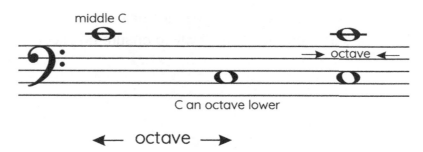

middle C

octave

C an octave lower

← octave →

Now that we know how to play octaves with both hands, let's discuss the octave symbol. When the composer wants you to play a series of notes an octave higher, they will sometimes use an octave *above* symbol with a line above all the notes that should be played an octave higher. The "a" in "8va" is used to represent an octave "above."

With the *8va* symbol, the notes below are what it should actually sound like

Conversely, when the composer wants you to play a series of notes an octave *lower*, they will use an octave *below* symbol with a line above all the notes that should be played an octave lower. The "b" in "8vb" is used to represent an octave "below."

With the *8vb* symbol, it should sound like the notes below. We haven't covered the bass clef notes yet, but they are basically the C Major scale notes sounding an octave lower, as seen below.

☐ Play a C Major scale an octave above middle C (as written below).

☐ Play a C Major scale an octave below middle C (as written below).

Video link: *https://www.musicmousestudios.com/piano-instructional-videos*

New Note B in Bass Clef

In the last lesson, we learned where B is in the Treble Clef. Today, we will be playing B in the Bass Clef.

☐ Playing exercise #1: Find middle C and then play it with your thumb.

☐ Playing exercise #2: Play the note next to middle C with your second finger. This is B. Refer to the picture below.

☐ Playing exercise #3: Now we will play the B an octave below the B you just played. Because we're playing an octave, we will use our thumb and pinky. Instead of using your second finger on B, shift your thumb over to that B. Now with your pinky, stretch it down to the B an octave below.

Video link: *https://www.musicmousestudios.com/piano-instructional-videos*

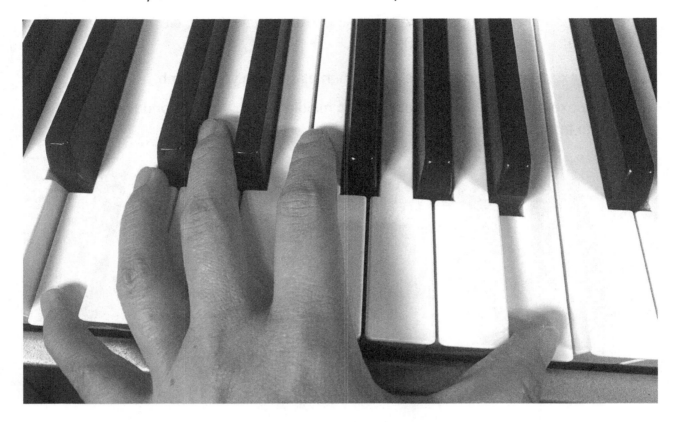

Now let's see what these B's look like on the Bass Clef staff. The space note that's above the top line is the B right below middle C. The B, an octave below middle C, is on the second line.

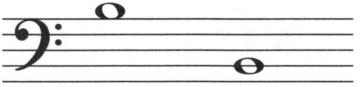

Played together as a stacked B octave chord, it looks like the following:

Music Notation Exercise

Since we are playing with our left hand, we need to draw a bass clef. As seen above, a bass clef looks like an F with 2 dots on the top 2 spaces of the staff.

☐ Draw a bass clef.

☐ Draw a middle C whole note.

☐ Draw a whole note on the C below middle C and stack it as an octave chord below the middle C you drew.

☐ Draw a whole note B (the B right below middle C).

☐ Draw a whole note B, an octave below the B you just drew, and stack it as an octave chord.

Rhythm Exercises

For each of the rhythm exercises below:

☐ Clap and count them aloud.

☐ Play them slowly on the piano.

Video link: *https://www.musicmousestudios.com/piano-instructional-videos*

Notice how the notes are all in octaves, either on C or B, with the octaves to be played with your pinky and thumb.

When we put the Treble Clef and Bass Clef staffs together and combine them with a **brace**, we form what's called the **Grand Staff**. The Grand Staff indicates that we play with both our right and left hands.

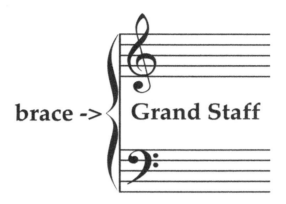

New Song: "Ode to Joy" (Both Hands)

You played this song in a previous lesson, but now we will add the left hand and play it together with the right hand!

☐ Write down all the letters below the music notes.

☐ Clap and count the rhythm of the right hand.

☐ Clap and count the rhythm of the left hand.

☐ Finger the right hand on the table (C with your thumb, D with your 2nd finger, E with your 3rd finger, F with your 4th finger, and G with your pinky).

☐ Finger the left hand on the table (All C and B octaves should be played with your pinky and thumb).

☐ Play this song slowly with your left hand first. You can move on to the right hand once you feel comfortable with your left.

☐ Play this song slowly with your right hand.

☐ Play this song slowly with hands together. OPTIONAL: You can speed it up once you have mastered it.

Video link: *https://www.musicmousestudios.com/piano-instructional-videos*

Ode to Joy

Ludwig van Beethoven
arr. by Andrea Chang

Congratulations, you've completed Lesson 9!

"Nothing is impossible.
The word itself says: 'I'm possible!'"

—AUDREY HEPBURN

LESSON
10
The Ambidextrous Mastery

The marvels of our brain never cease to amaze, enabling us to send neuro signals throughout our entire body, orchestrating the actions of various body parts. In the upcoming lesson, let's enhance our coordination skills and direct our attention toward achieving harmony between our left and right hands on the piano!

DAY 86 · Warmup Review

DAY 87 · New Note G in Bass Clef

☐ Play a C Major Scale (ascending and descending) with your right hand 5 times, starting at middle C.

☐ With your left hand, play C D E F G ascending and descending G F E D C 5 times. Practice slowly to ensure no sticky fingers!

In our warmups, we played C D E F G in our left hand. We will learn about that same G today. Like C and B from the last lesson, we can also play G an octave lower.

☐ Playing exercise #1: Find middle C and then play it with your thumb.

☐ Playing exercise #2: Keep your thumb on middle C and play down to your fourth finger. This is the G below middle C. Refer to the picture below.

☐ Playing exercise #3: Shift your 4th finger to your left **thumb** on the G below middle C, and stretch your pinky down to the G an octave below.

This is what the notes look like on the staff. Notice how these two G's make an **octave**. Like with other notes, they can be written arpeggiated as a melodic octave or stacked together like a chord as a harmonic octave.

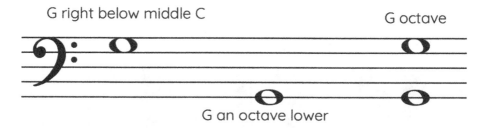

G right below middle C

G octave

G an octave lower

Video link: https://www.musicmousestudios.com/piano-instructional-videos

New Note A in Bass Clef

Previously, we learned how to play B in the bass clef. If we go one note down from B, we are at A.

☐ Playing exercise #1: Find middle C and then play it with your thumb.

☐ Playing exercise #2: Keep your thumb on middle C and play down to your third finger. This is the A below middle C. Refer to the picture below.

☐ Playing exercise #3: Now let's play the A an octave below the A you just played. Because we're playing an octave, we will use our pinky and thumb. Instead of using your 3rd finger on A, shift your thumb to that A. Now with your pinky, stretch it down to the A an octave below.

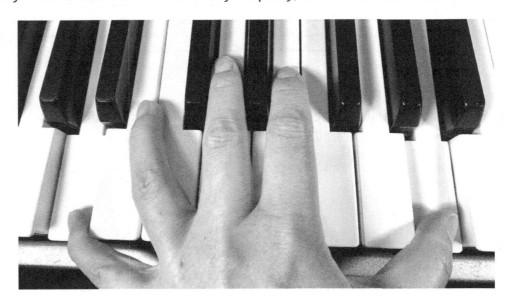

This is what the A's should look like on the staff.

Video link: *https://www.musicmousestudios.com/piano-instructional-videos*

Music Notation Exercise

☐ Draw a bass clef.

☐ Draw a whole note for the A below middle C.

☐ Draw a whole note for the A, an octave below that, and stack it below as an octave chord.

☐ Draw a whole note G below middle C.

☐ Draw the G an octave below that and stack it as an octave chord.

Rhythm Exercises

For each of the rhythm exercises below:

☐ Clap and count them aloud.

☐ Play them slowly on the piano.

Video link: https://www.musicmousestudios.com/piano-instructional-videos

Note: The first two exercises have octave chords on A or G.

The second two exercises have octave notes arpeggiated on A, G, C, or B.

All octaves should be played with your pinky and thumb.

When we have a repeated pattern of notes, like in Exercises 3 and 4, we call that an **ostinato.** Sometimes in piano, you will find ostinatos that occur in your left hand, which we will see in the next song we will be learning.

New Song: "Go Tell Aunt Rhody" (Both Hands)

We will continue playing "Go Tell Aunt Rhody" this week and add in the left hand! On Day 91, practice Part A; on Day 92, practice Part B; on Day 93, practice Part A and putting it together; on Day 94, solidify putting Part A, B, and A together and try to perform it for someone!

Video link: *https://www.musicmousestudios.com/piano-instructional-videos*

☐ Write down all the letters below the music notes.

☐ Clap and count the rhythm of the right hand.

☐ Clap and count the rhythm of the left hand.

☐ Fill out the rest of the fingering in the song. The right hand fingering is provided. The left hand fingering consists of octaves played as chords and arpeggios with the thumb and 5th finger.

☐ Finger the right hand on the table.

☐ Finger the left hand on the table.

☐ Finger both hands together on the table.

☐ Play this song slowly with your left hand first. You can move on to the right once you feel comfortable with your left hand.

☐ Play this song slowly with your right hand.

☐ Play this song slowly with both hands together. OPTIONAL: You can speed it up once you have mastered it.

Go Tell Aunt Rhody

for Piano

Jean-Jacques Rousseau
Arranged by Andrea Chang

Part A

Congratulations, you've completed Lesson 10!

"I can accept failure;
everyone fails at something.
But I can't accept not trying."

—MICHAEL JORDAN

LESSON
11
The Power of 3

Get ready to immerse yourself in the captivating realm of threes! In this upcoming lesson, we will delve into a fresh time signature and discover ties and a new rhythm that will broaden your rhythmic horizons!

C Major Scale Left Hand

To finger a C Major scale with your left hand, play the following notes with these fingers in this order:

Ascending

C (below middle C) – Finger 5

D (below middle C) – Finger 4

E (below middle C) – Finger 3

F (below middle C) – Finger 2

G (below middle C) – Finger 1

A (below middle C) – Finger 3 (cross over Finger 1)

B (below middle C) – Finger 2

C (middle C) – Finger 1

This is what your finger should look like going from G to A with the 3rd finger crossing over the thumb.

Today, we are only focusing on ascending. We will practice descending in another lesson.

Warmup Review

☐ Play a C Major Scale with your right hand (ascending and descending) 5 times.

☐ Play an ascending C Major Scale with your left hand 5 times. Practice slowly to ensure no sticky fingers!

Video link: *https://www.musicmousestudios.com/piano-instructional-videos*

Intervals Review

☐ Label these ascending intervals.

☐ Check your answers.

| 5th | 3rd | 4th | 2nd | 7th | octave | 6th | 3rd |

☐ Label these descending intervals.

☐ Check your answers.

| 2nd | 4th | octave | 7th | 5th | 3rd | 3rd | 6th |

☐ Label these interval chords.

☐ Check your answers.

octave 6th 2nd 7th   3rd 4th 5th

☐ Fill in the missing **top** note to create these interval chords.

5th 3rd 4th 2nd   7th octave 6th

☐ Check your answers.

5th 3rd 4th 2nd   7th octave 6th

☐ Fill in the missing **bottom** note to create these interval chords.

example: 3rd 2nd 4th   7th 5th 6th
octave

☐ Check your answers.

example: 3rd 2nd 4th   7th 5th 6th
octave

Dotted Half Note

Today, we're learning a new rhythm called a dotted half note! Its name is derived from the fact that it consists of a half note followed by a dot. A dotted half note is held for 3 beats.

¾ Time Signature

All the music we've been playing thus far has been in the time signature 4/4. Today, we will explore a new time signature, 3/4. As previously mentioned, in a time signature, the top number tells us how many beats are in a measure, and the bottom number tells us the unit of time or which note receives one beat. In 3/4, the 3 on top tells us that there are 3 beats per measure, and the 4 on the bottom signifies that the quarter note gets the beat.

 # beats per measure
There are 3 beats per a measure
What note gets 1 beat?
When 4's on the bottom, quarter
gets 1 beat

3/4 feels a lot different than 4/4. Songs written in 3/4 often include waltzes, where you really feel that first beat in the 3-beat pattern.

Dotted half notes frequently occur in 3/4. We will look at a song today that uses both 3/4 and dotted half notes.

Play These Dotted Half Notes!

☐ Label all the letters underneath the notes.

☐ Play the exercise below using the fingering provided.

Video link: *https://www.musicmousestudios.com/piano-instructional-videos*

When you want notes to sustain for longer than their expected duration, you can add a **tie** and connect it to the following note. For example, if I had a dotted half note and I wanted that note to be 2 beats longer, I would tie a half note next to that dotted half note. This tie signifies that you will hold the duration of the first note (dotted half note) in addition to the duration of the second note (half note). Let's clap and count some examples below:

1   In this first example, you will hold the note for 6 beats total (3 beats for the first measure tied to 3 beats in the second measure). Try clapping and counting this (you will only clap once and hold that clap for 6 beats).

Video link: *https://www.musicmousestudios.com/piano-instructional-videos*

2   Notice how ties can face upward (like in the previous example) or downward (like in the example below). They will generally follow the opposite direction of the stems of the notes they tie together. In this second example, you will hold the note for 5 beats total (3 beats for the first measure and 2 beats for the second measure). Try clapping and counting this!

3   In this third example, you will hold the note for 4 beats total (3 beats for the first measure and 1 beat for the second measure). Try clapping and counting this!

4 In this fourth example, you will hold the note for 3.5 beats total (3 beats for the first measure and 1/2 beat for the second measure). Try clapping and counting this!

How Many Beats?

Fill in the blanks with the total number of beats you should hold each tie for.

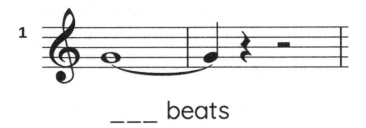

1

_____ beats

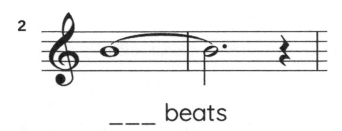

2

_____ beats

3

_____ beats

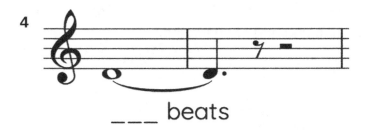

4

_____ beats

5

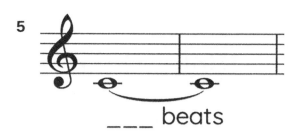

___ beats

6

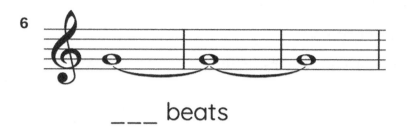

___ beats

Answers

1 5 beats

2 7 beats

3 6 beats

4 5.5 beats

5 8 beats

6 12 beats

New Song:
"Amazing Grace" – Right Hand

Today, we will learn just the right hand to "Amazing Grace."

☐ Write down all the letters below the music notes.

☐ Circle the time signature of the song. How many beats are in a measure? Which note gets the beat?

☐ Circle any ties you see in the song.

☐ Clap and count the rhythm. It should sound like the following.

Video link: https://www.musicmousestudios.com/piano-instructional-videos

☐ Finger the music on the table to the rhythm you just clapped. Follow the fingering provided.

Amazing Grace
for Piano

John Newton
Arranged by Andrea Chang

☐ Play this song slowly. OPTIONAL: You can speed it up once you have mastered it.

John Newton, the author behind the timeless hymn "Amazing Grace," was born in London in 1725. He grew up at sea, sailing alongside his father, starting at the age of 11. His mother brought him up in Christianity as a child, but her untimely death when Newton was at the tender age of seven caused him to largely forsake his faith. Newton began working on slave ships and eventually became Captain of several of them. Sailing around Africa, he sought out and captured slaves and sold them to make a profit.

One fateful day, he encountered a ferocious storm. Some of his crew went overboard, and their ship was on the brink of sinking. As Newton frantically tried to steer the ship, he shouted, "Lord, have mercy on us!" After 11 hours of continuing to struggle, Newton finally got the

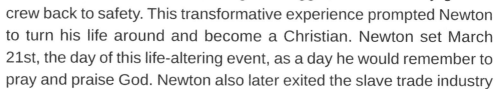

crew back to safety. This transformative experience prompted Newton to turn his life around and become a Christian. Newton set March 21st, the day of this life-altering event, as a day he would remember to pray and praise God. Newton also later exited the slave trade industry and fervently advocated for the abolition of slavery. He then learned Hebrew and Greek and became ordained as a pastor, leading his own church.

In 1767, a poet named William Cowper, who frequented Newton's church, collaborated with Newton to create a remarkable collection of hymns, which came to be known as the *Olney Hymns*. This volume was published in 1779, and nestled within its pages lay the verses of "Amazing Grace," initially titled "Faith's Review and Expectation."

Congratulations, you've completed Lesson 11!

"Tough times never last, but tough people do."

—ROBERT H. SCHULLER

LESSON
12
Harmonic Horizons

In our upcoming lesson, we will dig deeply into the realm of
chords to expand your understanding of harmonics!

C Major Scale Left Hand

To finger a descending C Major scale with your left hand, play the following notes with these fingers in this order:

Descending

C (middle C) – Finger 1

B (below middle C) – Finger 2

A (below middle C) – Finger 3

G (below middle C) – Finger 1

F (below middle C) – Finger 2

E (below middle C) – Finger 3

D (below middle C) – Finger 4

C (below middle C) – Finger 5

This is what your finger should look like going from A to G with the thumb crossing under the 3rd finger.

Warmup Review

For the following, practice slowly to ensure no sticky fingers!

☐ Play a descending C Major Scale with your left hand 5 times.

☐ Play an ascending C Major Scale followed by a descending C Major Scale with your left hand 5 times.

☐ Play a C Major Scale with your right hand, ascending and descending 5 times.

☐ Play a C Major scale ascending and descending with both hands.

Video link: https://www.musicmousestudios.com/piano-instructional-videos

New Note D in Bass Clef

Today, we will learn where D is on the piano and on the staff.

☐ Playing exercise #1: Find the D above middle C and play it with your thumb.

☐ Playing exercise #2: Stretch your pinky an octave below that D and play it simultaneously with the higher D. Refer to the picture below.

Video link: https://www.musicmousestudios.com/piano-instructional-videos

This is what the notes look like on the staff.

D above middle C   D an octave
below middle C   D octave

Music Notation Exercise

☐ On the staff below, draw a bass clef.

☐ Draw the D above middle C.

☐ Draw the D an octave below that D and stack it as an octave chord.

Chord Structures

In a scale, certain notes are essential for making a chord. These notes are 1, 3, and 5. A three-note chord is called a **triad**.

Let's take the C Major scale that we have been playing. **Note:** This is NOT fingering numbers. This is simply the notes labeled by the order they come on the scale. For example, C will be 1 because it's the first note in the C Major scale. D will be 2 because it's the second note in the scale, and so and so forth.

C – 1

D – 2

E – 3

F – 4

G – 5

A – 6

B – 7

☐ Circle the 1, 3, and 5 notes above.

The 1, 3, and 5 notes in a C Major scale are C, E, and G. We can use these to build a triad. We can also rearrange the 1, 3, and 5 notes in different orders to create variations of C Major chords. Each of these variations has a name.

When 1 is on the bottom of the triad, we say this chord is in **root** position. When 3 is on the bottom, the chord is in **first inversion**. When 5 is on the bottom, the chord is in **second inversion**. We can apply this to chords both in the treble and the bass clef.

Sometimes, notes from the triad (out of 1, 3, 5) can be missing. However, we can still deduce that the chord is in C Major since it is implied by the presence of the other notes in the triad, as seen in the last three chords of the row. Notice also how in the second inversion chord in the bass clef, the top note is an E, a note we haven't covered yet, but if you count up from middle C, it is on the ledger line right above it. Refer to the picture below for all the different chord inversions of C Major.

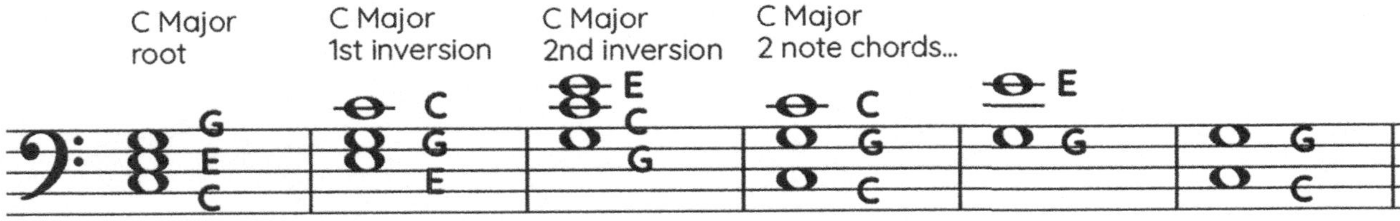

Chord Playing Exercises

Review the C Major chords from the last lesson and familiarize yourself with the notes. Let's try playing some of these chords below. If you'd like, write the letter notes in the exercises below to reinforce them. Follow the fingering provided.

Video link: https://www.musicmousestudios.com/piano-instructional-videos

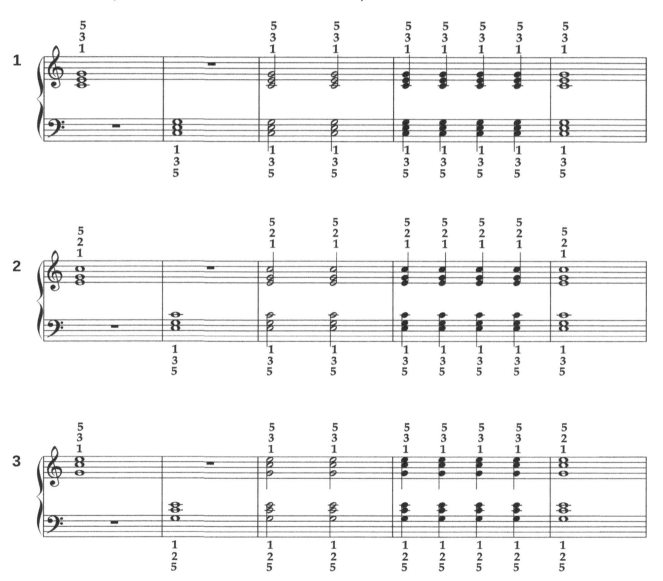

Chord Playing Exercises

DAY
108-109

We can also apply this to other starting notes. For example, if G is our root note, then we are in the key of G Major. We would label all of the letters of the scale in G Major as the following:

G – 1

A – 2

B – 3

C – 4

D – 5

E – 6

F♯ (we will cover what ♯ is in the next lesson) – 7

The 1, 3, and 5 notes are G, B, and D. Knowing this, we can also play through the various inversions of a G Major chord (root, 1st, 2nd, and those with missing notes), as seen in the picture below.

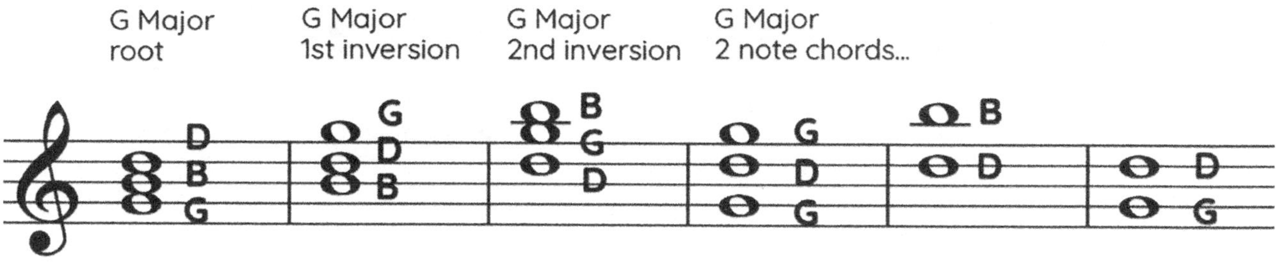

Refer to the G Major chords above and familiarize yourself with the notes. Let's try playing some of these exercises. If you'd like, write down the letter notes in the exercises below to further reinforce them. Follow the fingering provided.

Video link: *https://www.musicmousestudios.com/piano-instructional-videos*

Music Notation Exercises

☐ On the first staff below, draw a treble clef and C Major root, 1st inversion, and 2nd inversion chords.

☐ On the second staff below, draw a bass clef and C Major root, 1st inversion, and 2nd inversion chords.

☐ On the third staff below, draw a treble clef and G Major root, 1st inversion, and 2nd inversion chords.

☐ On the fourth staff below, draw a bass clef and G Major root, 1st inversion, and 2nd inversion chords.

Today we will put the left and right hand together to "Amazing Grace!" Notice how in the left hand, even though there are 3 notes, they consist of 2 letter notes, creating the "implied" G Major chords we discussed earlier.

- ☐ Write down all the letters above or below the music notes.

- ☐ Circle the time signature of the song. How many beats are in a measure? Which note gets the beat?

- ☐ Circle any ties you see in the song.

Video link: https://www.musicmousestudios.com/piano-instructional-videos

- ☐ Clap and count the rhythm of the right hand.

- ☐ Clap and count the rhythm of the left hand.

- ☐ Clap and count the rhythm of both hands on the table.

- ☐ Finger the right hand on the table. Follow the fingering provided.

- ☐ Finger the left hand on the table. You will be using the same fingering for each chord in the song, so from the bottom to top, the fingers 5, 2, and 1, respectively, will be used to play each chord in the song.

- ☐ Finger the song with both hands on the table.

- ☐ Play this song slowly with your left hand first.

- ☐ Play this song slowly with your right hand.

- ☐ Play this song slowly with hands together. OPTIONAL: You can speed it up once you have mastered it.

Amazing Grace

for Piano

John Newton
Arranged by Andrea Chang

Repeat Sign Symbols

If you are familiar with the song "Amazing Grace," you may have noticed that it contains multiple verses, as seen in the music below (on Day 115). **Repeat signs** are placed at the beginning and end of the sections the composer wishes to repeat to save space and avoid duplicating the same music for each verse. In the case of "Amazing Grace," the entire song is repeated because there are repeat symbols at the beginning and the end of the piece. This practice is commonly found in hymns, where the lyrics for each verse are listed in between the staffs, and a repeat sign is used to indicate that the same music should be played for each verse. A repeat sign consists of two dots placed in the middle two spaces of the staff. The beginning repeat sign appears before two bar lines, while the ending repeat sign is followed by two bar lines.

1st and 2nd Endings

Additionally, in the music below, you may have noticed other markings at the end of the piece, specifically brackets with numbers inside, positioned above the last two measures. The first bracket contains the numbers 1, 2, and 3 and indicate different endings for the piece, known as 1st and 2nd Endings, depending on how many times the music has been repeated. In our case, during the first three repetitions of the piece, you will play the same ending, as indicated in measure 16 (the measure with the bracket displaying 1, 2, 3 above it). On the fourth repetition of the piece, you will skip measure 16 and play measure 17 instead (the final measure with the bracket and the number 4 on top of it).

New Song: "Amazing Grace"
(Multiple Verses)

Amazing Grace
for Piano

John Newton
Arranged by Andrea Chang

- [ ] Circle where the repeat signs are.

- [ ] Play Amazing Grace through all its verses using the repeat signs and 1st, 2nd, 3rd, and 4th endings.

- [ ] Perform this for someone or share this with us on our website!

Video link: *https://www.musicmousestudios.com/piano-instructional-videos*

☐ Play a C Major Scale with both hands ascending and descending 5 times.

New Note E in Bass Clef

Today, we will learn the last two notes in the bass clef – E and F.

☐ Playing exercise #1: Find the E above middle C and play it with your left thumb.

☐ Playing exercise #2: Stretch your pinky an octave below that E and play it simultaneously as the higher E. Refer to the picture below.

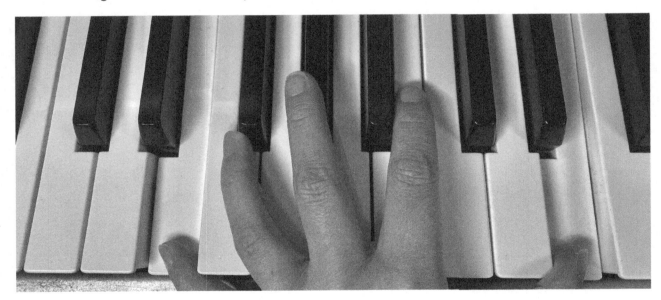

Below is what E looks like written out on the staff. The first chord on the left is what we just played on the piano. Because this chord is a bit higher (notice the ledger line E on top, you may prefer to play it an octave lower, which is the chord displayed in the staff on the right.

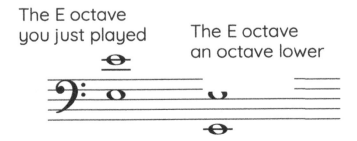

The E octave you just played

The E octave an octave lower

Video link: https://www.musicmousestudios.com/piano-instructional-videos

New Note F in Bass Clef

Now, for the final white note in our left hand… we will learn F!

☐ Playing exercise #1: Find the F above middle C and play it with your left thumb.

☐ Playing exercise #2: Stretch your pinky an octave below that F and play it at the same time as the higher F. Refer to the picture below.

Below is what F looks like on the staff. The first chord on the left is what we just played on the piano. Because this chord is a bit higher (notice the ledger line F on top, you may prefer to play it an octave lower, which is the chord displayed in the staff on the right.

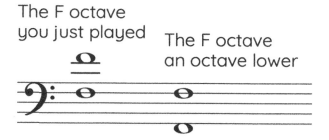

The F octave you just played

The F octave an octave lower

Video link: *https://www.musicmousestudios.com/piano-instructional-videos*

Notes Acronyms: Memorization Tips for Bass Clef Notes

Now that we've covered all of the white notes in the bass clef, you can use any of the acronyms below to remember the **line notes** GBDFA in the Bass Clef. Choose your favorite!

Good	Boys	Do	Fine	Always
Good	Bikes	Don't	Fall	Apart
Grizzly	Bears	Don't	Fly	Airplanes

To easily remember the **space notes** A C E G in the Bass Clef, you can use the simple mnemonic "All Cows Eat Grass."

All   Cows   Eat   Grass

Name that Note!

Let's review all of the notes in the treble and bass clefs. Write the letter names below.

Performance (OPTIONAL)

Practice all of the songs and perform them for someone or share it with us on our website, www.musicmousestudios.com!

☐ Mary Had a Little Lamb

☐ Down the River

☐ Oh When the Saints Go Marching In

☐ Twinkle, Twinkle Little Star

☐ The Amazing Twinkle, Twinkle Little Star

☐ Ode to Joy

☐ Go Tell Aunt Rhody

☐ Amazing Grace

Congratulations, you've completed Lesson 12!

"It always seems impossible until it's done."

—NELSON MANDELA

CERTIFICATE
OF AWARD

presented to :

Congratulations! You have graduated from Book 1 -
Your Golden Ears: First Piano Lessons for Adult Beginners!

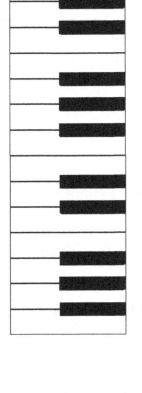

Andrea Chang

Founder of
Music Mouse Studios

_____
Date

Leave A 1-Click Review!

I would be incredibly thankful if you could just take 60 seconds to write a brief review on Amazon, even if it's just a few sentences.

Customer reviews

 5 out of 5

2 global ratings

5 star	████████████	100%
4 star		0%
3 star		0%
2 star		0%
1 star		0%

⌄ How customer reviews and ratings work

Review this product

Share your thoughts with other customers

Conclusion – Beyond the Last Note

Congratulations, you did it!!! That was not an easy feat completing this course, but you preserved and nailed it!! We have covered a wide range of essential topics, including selecting the right piano or keyboard for your needs and exploring various options available. You have learned how to confidently navigate the piano, playing and reading notes in both your left and right hands. The basics of music theory have been demystified, enabling you to understand the structure and elements of music.

We have also focused on honing your technical skills and finger dexterity through our carefully crafted warmups and playing exercises. By practicing these exercises, you have developed the foundation necessary for playing more complex pieces with confidence and precision. Additionally, we have delved into the realm of music analysis and music theory, empowering you to appreciate and interpret compositions with a deeper understanding.

Furthermore, this book has allowed you to explore the enchanting world of classical music. You have been introduced to timeless masterpieces and had the opportunity to learn about the fascinating backgrounds of renowned composers. By connecting with their stories, you have gained a greater appreciation for the rich history and emotions encapsulated within each musical work.

As you conclude this book, remember that your journey as a pianist is just beginning! It is crucial to continue learning, practicing, and pushing your boundaries. Don't be discouraged by challenges; instead, see them as stepping stones to growth and improvement. You now possess the tools and knowledge to apply what you have learned, and this book will serve as a valuable resource you can always refer back to.

Put into practice all that you have learned and persistently pursue excellence in your piano playing. Embrace the opportunity to apply your knowledge, honing your skills with dedication and a commitment to continuous improvement. Your journey toward mastery awaits, and we believe in your ability to achieve greatness in your musical endeavors! Share your progress with us, inspire others, and continue to pursue your musical dreams with passion and determination!!

If you have found value in this book, we kindly ask for your support. Please consider leaving a positive review on Amazon and subscribing to our YouTube channel, where you will find more valuable content and piano lessons! Visit us at https://www.youtube.com/@homeschoolingwithandrea.

For personalized assistance, additional resources, and support, we invite you to explore our website, *www.musicmousestudios.com*. You will find a wealth of information to aid you on your musical journey.

And don't forget about your free gift!

To receive this exclusive download of additional sheet music and songs, simply visit *https://www.musicmousestudios.com/contact* **and include the text "SHEET MUSIC" in your message.**

We have thoroughly enjoyed being a part of your piano journey so far, and we are excited to continue supporting you as you grow and excel as a pianist. The best is yet to come!

Keep playing, keep learning,
and keep reaching for the stars!

References

Sarah Josepha Hale: The Godmother of Thanksgiving. (n.d.). Almanac.com. https://www.almanac. com/sarah-josepha-hale-godmother-thanksgiving#:~:text=In%201863%2C%20with%20 the%20country,Lincoln%20liked%20Hale's%20idea.

Wikipedia contributors. (2023). Sarah Josepha Hale. *Wikipedia*. https://en.wikipedia.org/wiki/ Sarah_Josepha_Hale

Amelinckx, A. (2018, October 2). *The True Story Behind "Mary Had a Little Lamb" – Modern Farmer.* Modern Farmer. https://modernfarmer.com/2017/12/ true-story-behind-mary-little-lamb/

Wikipedia contributors. (2023b). Ludwig van Beethoven. *Wikipedia*. https://en.m.wikipedia.org/ wiki/Ludwig_van_Beethoven

Ludwig van Beethoven | Biography, Music, & Facts. (2023, April 25). Encyclopedia Britannica. https://www.britannica.com/biography/Ludwig-van-Beethoven/Early-influences

The remarkable story of Beethoven's 'Choral' Symphony No. 9 and the 'Ode to Joy.' (n.d.). Classic FM. https://www.classicfm.com/composers/beethoven/music/symphony-no-9-d-minor/

Wikipedia contributors. (2023c). Helene von Breuning. *Wikipedia*. https://en.m.wikipedia.org/wiki/ Helene_von_Breuning

Wikipedia contributors. (2023a). Jane Taylor (poet). *Wikipedia*. https://en.wikipedia.org/wiki/ Jane_Taylor_(poet)

Wikipedia contributors. (2001). Jean-Jacques Rousseau. *Wikipedia*. https://en.wikipedia.org/wiki/ Jean-Jacques_Rousseau

Hymnology: The Story Behind "Amazing Grace" – Geneva College. (n.d.). https://www.geneva. edu/blog/uncategorized/hymnology-amazing-grace#:~:text=It%20was%20December%20 1772%2C%20in,him%20out%20of%20his%20wretchedness.

Petruzzello, M. (2021, December 13). *John Newton | Biography, Conversion, Hymns, Abolition, & Facts.* Encyclopedia Britannica. https://www.britannica.com/biography/John-Newton

Wikipedia contributors. (2023f). John Newton. *Wikipedia*. https://en.m.wikipedia.org/wiki/ John_Newton

Choosing a Piano:Grand or Upright? – Musical Instrument Guide – Yamaha Corporation. (n.d.). https://www.yamaha.com/en/musical_instrument_guide/piano/selection/#:~:text=In%20 an%20upright%20piano%2C%20the,a%20greater%20potential%20for%20expression.

Bradfield Piano Restoration, Moving & Storage. (2022). Grand Piano vs. Baby Grand Piano. *Bradfield Piano Restoration, Moving & Storage.* https://bradfieldpiano.com/grand-vs-baby-grand-piano/#:~:text=Some%20piano%20manufacturers%20may%20classify,grand%20piano%20longer%20than%207%E2%80%B3.

200+ Motivational Quotes To Inspire and Win 2023. (2022, December 1). Shopify. https://www.shopify.com/blog/motivational-quotes

Liles, M. (2023, March 9). Stay Motivated When the Going Gets Tough Thanks to These 100 Quotes About Not Giving Up. Parade: Entertainment, Recipes, Health, Life, Holidays. https://parade.com/980122/marynliles/not-giving-up-quotes/

117 Never Give Up Quotes (+ My 5 Favorite Tips to Help You Keep Going). (2022, April 25). The Positivity Blog. https://www.positivityblog.com/never-give-up-quotes/

Edinburgh, K. (2023). 55 Uplifting Quotes to Encourage Making Progress. Exam Study Expert. https://examstudyexpert.com/progress-quotes/#quotes-to-help-you-get-a-new-perspective-on-your-progress

You Can Do It Quotes. (n.d.). BrainyQuote. https://www.brainyquote.com/topics/you-can-do-it-quotes

Made in the USA
Middletown, DE
22 January 2024